D1073978

THE MIRACULOUS JOURNEY OF MAHOMET

THE MIRACULOUS JOURNEY OF MAHOMET

Mirâj Nâmeh

BIBLIOTHÈQUE NATIONALE, PARIS

(Manuscrit Supplément Turc 190)

INTRODUCTION AND COMMENTARIES BY

MARIE-ROSE SÉGUY

George Braziller *New York*

Reproduced from the Illuminated Manuscript (*Supplément Turc 190*)
Belonging to the Bibliothèque Nationale, Paris, France

Translated from the French by Richard Pevear

Published in 1977

George Braziller, Inc.
One Park Avenue, New York, N.Y. 10016

Library of Congress Catalog Number: 0-8076-0868-8
International Standard Book Number: 77-5140
Printed in France by Draeger, Paris
Bound in Switzerland by Mayer & Soutter

BOOK DESIGN BY VINCENT TORRE

CONTENTS

INTRODUCTION

The Manuscript

THE *Mirâj Nâmeh* is a mystical legend describing the marvellous or apocalyptical visions that marked the stages of the miraculous ascension in the course of which, one night, the founder of Islam reached the Throne of God.

This manuscript of the *Mirâj*, translated into eastern Turkish by the poet Mîr Haydar, was calligraphed by Mâlik Bakhshî of Herât in the Uighur script. It is decorated with sixty-one illuminations, which bring before our by turns amazed and anguished eyes the successive stages of the prodigious journey of Mahomet (or Muhammad), first through the heavenly regions interwoven of gold and blue and peopled with angels with multicolored wings, and then through the infernal world of shadows haunted by demons who torture the damned.

Produced in the 15th century, this masterwork from the illumination workshops of Herât, in Khurasan, was purchased on Thursday, the fourteenth of January, 1673, in Constantinople, by the famous translator of the *Thousand-and-One Nights*, Antoine Galland (1646–1715). Having twice led scientific missions to the Levant, this French orientalist had acquired a profound knowledge of the language, customs, and literatures of the Middle Eastern peoples. His erudition enabled him to assemble a valuable collection of Arabic, Turkish, and Persian manuscripts, among them the *Mirâj Nâmeh*, which he purchased for Charles-François Olier, Marquis de Nointel, then French ambassador to Constantinople. Brought back to France, this unique manuscript was placed in the Colbert Library. The minister of Louis XIV was an inquisitive bibliophile and asked François Pétis de la Croix (1653–1713) to produce a review of the book. However, despite his functions as secretary-interpreter to the King, and the training he had acquired as an orientalist in the course of travels to Egypt, the Holy Land, Persia, Armenia, and Constantinople, Pétis de la Croix had to admit his inability to decipher a text whose language he could not even identify. Nevertheless, he set down a description of the paintings decorating the work and made an attempt to translate its Turkish inscriptions. Toward the middle of the 18th century, the manuscript was deposited in the Royal Library. It was not until almost a century and a half after its acquisition that an eminent sinologist, Abel Rémusat (1788–1832) succeeded in deciphering some fragments of the text, whose existence he immediately announced on page 252 of his famous *Recherches sur les langues tartares (Studies of the Tartar Languages)*, published in 1820: "There is in the Royal Library a folio manuscript written . . . in Uighur script. The subject of this work is theological; it contains . . . the story of the *Mirâj* or fabulous ascension of Mahomet. . . ." Today this invaluable manuscript is catalogued in the Bibliothèque Nationale as number 190 in the supplement of the Turkish collection.

The story of Mahomet's journey takes up the first sixty-eight pages of the volume. The text of this narrative is followed by another work, also in Uighur script, known as the *Memorial of the Saints*. The colophon at the end tells us that the text was written out in Herât, in the 840th year of the Hegira, a date which corresponds to the year 1436 of the Christian era.

Herât, capital of Khurasan, became at the beginning of the 15th century the residence of Shah Rokh. He remained there for almost half a century (1404–1447). The brilliance of his court, further enhanced by a galaxy of thinkers, poets, painters, and musicians, made his reign one of the brightest periods in the history of Khurasan. In the royal studios attached to the court, calligraphers, illuminators, and bookbinders produced manuscripts a number of which found a place in the vast and famous library the sovereign, Shah Rokh, had assembled.

The account of the *Mirâj* contained in this manuscript was translated into eastern Turkish from an Arabic original by Mîr Haydar—a poet and man of letters known for his irresistible mystical bent—and was calligraphed in Uighur script by Mâlik Bakhshî of Herât. The paintings that illustrate the story, most likely the work of several artists, are accompanied by marginal notes in Arabic and Turkish, and on the upper parts of certain sheets there are traces of Persian captions.

Uighur script, derived from an old Aramaic alphabet, was spread through Central Asia by Manichaean missionaries who came from Sogdiana. For many centuries it served as medium for the first literary works in the Turkish language.

Descendants of the Huns and related to the Turks, the Uighurs, according to the Chinese Annals, had exercised hegemony over Upper Asia from 744 to 840 and had founded a brilliant empire in which Manichaeism brought this warlike people under the spiritual influence of Iran and enabled them to build a civilization of high cultural development, which was not without consequence for the evolution of the Turco-Mongol peoples in the 9th to 13th centuries.

The Ascension of the Prophet

Inspired by the first verse of *al-Isra sura* (XVII) of the Koran (which says specifically: "Glory to Him Who carried His Servant by night from the Sacred Mosque at Mecca to the Remote Temple in Jerusalem whose precincts we blessed . . ."), this *Night Journey* is described as an ascension in the course of which Mahomet is led by the angel Gabriel from the "Sacred Mosque" at Mecca to the "Far-off Mosque" located in Jerusalem, and from there as far as the seventh Heaven where the Founder of Islam is admitted to ecstatic contemplation of the divine Essence. From the earliest centuries of the Hegira, this account had given rise to popular Arab stories, then to theological, mystical, or literary elaborations which, little by little, were integrated into Moslem eschatological beliefs based on the notion of the Last Judgment.

As a great prophet of the biblical line, Mahomet saw his mission confirmed on the grand and wonderful night of the *Mirâj*, in the course of which the founder of Islam was miraculously transported to the foot of the Throne of God. Coming from the semitic tribe of the Qoraish—who claimed descent from Ishmael, son of Abraham and Hajar—Mahomet "the Praised One" was born at Mecca in the year of the Elephant (ca. 570 A.D.). Tradition says that his prophetic mission began in 612. At that time, the future Chosen of God, weary of human incomprehension, had taken the habit of retreating to a hill a few miles from Mecca to meditate, pray, and practice an ascetic life. It was during the last ten days of Ramadan, in a grotto on Mount Hirā, on the "Blessed Night," that the angel Gabriel appeared to Mahomet, holding a scroll covered with writing and communicating to him the order to "recite," that is, "reveal," what was transmitted to him by the intermediary of the divine Spirit. Following the angel, the Prophet then recited words which penetrated and illuminated his being. Mahomet understood that Allah had chosen him to be his chief servant, sent by Him to transmit to the world the revelations he would receive, in fragments, from a heavenly messenger, the angel Gabriel. From this moment on, it was with an attitude of perfect submission and the most profound humility that he received the divine Word and transmitted it in total integrity. Put into writing, grouped by chapters (or *suras*) and arranged chronologically, these revelations became the sacred text of Islam, the Koran.

The ascension of Mahomet came a few years after the start of his prophetic mission, at a moment when the Prophet seemed abandoned by all and sundry but remained unswervingly obedient to the divine will. The event became the subject of marvellous accounts in which legend borders on ecstasy. As with all authentic spiritual experiences of the great mystics, it is by refraining from rationalist judgment that one can follow the successive episodes of this miraculous journey. There are significant variants among the many accounts; what follows is the version most commonly told and which is illustrated in the manuscript at the Bibliothèque Nationale.[1]

It was midsummer. During the twenty-seventh night of the seventh month of the year 620[?],[2] overcome with solitude, worry, and perhaps even anguish, Mahomet slept in a house not far from the sanctuary of the Kaaba (Plate 2). Suddenly the archangel Gabriel entered the sleeping Prophet's room. He set about first to purify his heart, washing his breast with water from the sacred spring of Zamzam[3] to remove all traces of error and doubt, idolatry and paganism. Then, taking up a golden beaker, he poured over him the *hikma,* symbolic of wisdom and faith. Covering his breast again, the angel took the Prophet's hand and helped him onto a mysterious mount, the *Burāq*, a fabulous animal as swift as lightning. And they departed, first on the earthly journey, the *isra,* to Jerusalem (Plate 3). After the traditional stops (not illustrated in our manuscript) at Mount Sinai, where Moses received the Tables of the Law, at the tomb of Abraham in Hebron, and at the birthplace of Jesus in Bethlehem, the Prophet, guided by Gabriel, arrives at the Holy City and enters the sanctuary of the "Remote Mosque" (Plate 4), where he is welcomed by a number of prophets with Abraham, Moses, and Jesus at their head. There Mahomet leads the common prayer (Plate 5). The Koran (*sura* XVII, verse 1) mentions this far-off Mosque, the last step of the *isra* and the point of departure of the *Mirâj*, the heavenly journey. And just as Abraham left his footprint at Mecca, so before undertaking the second stage of his ascent to the Eternal, Mahomet leaves his footprint on the Rock over which the "Dome of the Rock" will be built in the Holy City.

Then begins the flight to the first of the seven Heavens. (The existence of seven celestial spheres is mentioned in the Koran, *sura* LXVII, verse 3.) But before reaching the first of these spheres, the Prophet, riding the *Burâq* and guided by the archangel, sees a stairway of light starting from the earth and ending in Heaven. Having crossed it, Mahomet comes to the banks of the Kawthar (Plate 6), shown as an immense sea of which God alone knows the full extent and into which the rivers of Paradise flow. Pursuing his way across the sky (Plate 7), he comes to the first heaven, made of turquoise, where he meets the father of the human race, Adam (Plate 8), surrounded by his descendants, who are divided into two groups: to his right, the saved, on whom he smiles; to his left, the damned, who sadden him so much that he weeps while looking at them. Continuing across the first Heaven, Mahomet meets the angel in charge of counting the hours of the day and night. This heavenly creature is generally portrayed as a White Cock whose head grazes the Throne of God and whose feet rest on the earth (Plate 9). Further on, Mahomet finds himself in the presence of an angel made half of fire and half of snow (Plate 10), whose voice is so resounding when he recites the *Tesbih* that it echoes like thunder.

Guided by Gabriel, the Prophet goes through the doorway to the second Heaven, made of white pearls (Plate 11), and sees first an angel of gigantic proportions (Plate 12), then a many-headed angel whose seventy faces each have seventy tongues (Plate 13, upper part). In this Heaven dwell the prophets Zaccharias and his son John (Plate 13, lower part).

Continuing on his fantastic ride (Plate 14), he flies over the banks of a White Sea and reaches the third Heaven, made of red hyacinth, where stand thirty divisions of archangels with thirty thousand angels ready to serve each one of them. There he meets the prophets Jacob and his son Joseph (Plate

16), then David and Solomon (Plate 17), who greet him. Further on, he sees a colossal angel, also with seventy heads, sitting on the shore of an immense sea (Plate 18).

Coming then to the fourth Heaven, Mahomet is first greeted (as he has been in each of the preceding Heavens) by the angel who guards the door and by multitudes of angelic beings (Plate 19). At the entrance to each new heavenly sphere, Gabriel knocks at the door and is welcomed by an angel who is charged with protecting each Heaven against the assaults and curiosity of demons.

Continuing his tour, always guided by the archangel, he comes to the threshold of the fifth Heaven, which is made of gold. Having crossed over it, Mahomet sees four great biblical prophets: Ishmael, Isaac, Aaron, and Lot, who, upon seeing him, cry out: "O Muhammad! this night all that you ask of God will be granted without exception. Ask of Him salvation for the souls of your believers!" (Plate 20, upper part). Pushing further on, he sees a sea of fire (Plate 20, lower part). The angel Gabriel tells him that on the day of Resurrection this sea will be poured into Hell where it will cause the torments of the damned.

Coming then to the sixth Heaven, made of pearls, he is welcomed first by sixty divisions of angels singing litanies of the divine Names (Plate 21), then by the great biblical prophet Moses, surrounded by a host of his followers (Plate 23). Here occurs the episode in which the great Hebrew prophet weeps, realizing that the Moslem elect far outnumber the elect among his own people. But the Eternal, addressing Moses, reminds him that the benefits he had received to overflowing demanded rather that he offer God acts of thanksgiving. Pursuing his course, Mahomet finds himself next in the presence of the prophets Noah and Idris (Plate 24). The latter is named twice in the Koran, where he is described as a just man and a prophet. He would seem to be Enoch of the Bible, to whom legendary literature ascribes immortality. This pious man, sometimes made into a solar hero, had been miraculously lifted up to the Eternal at the age of 365.

After receiving the blessings of the latter two prophets, Mahomet takes up his way again toward the seventh Heaven, made of light. Having reached it, he is welcomed by the angel at the door (Plate 25), and then by seventy divisions of archangels. Then he notices a palace in front of him, with a throne (*minbar*) resting against it, and seated on the throne his ancestor, the prophet Abraham (Plate 26), who, answering Mahomet's greeting, says to him: "O Prophet of Prophets, welcome! God bless your arrival!" Invited by Abraham, he goes into the building where, he is told, seventy thousand angels come each day. Before the building he finds two groups of Moslems: those in the first group are dressed in white; the others wear white tunics striped with black (Plate 27). Speaking only to the wearers of white tunics, the angel Gabriel grants them permission to go in with the Prophet. Having moved on, Mahomet sees a Black Sea surrounded by shadows from which a numberless host of angelic beings emerge. On the shore stands a gigantic angel capable of swallowing the seven levels of the earth; his head touches the Throne of God and his feet rest on the ground (Plate 28). Not far away, another angel, as large as the earthly world, who has seventy heads, each with seventy mouths and each mouth with seventy tongues, sings litanies night and day in praise of the divine Name (Plate 29). Beside him stands another colossal angel with eyes so large that all the seas of the world would not fill them, and with ten thousand wings. When he dives into the waves and comes up shaking his wings, each drop of water that flies from them is miraculously transformed into a celestial spirit. Continuing on, Mahomet comes to a four-headed angel whose four faces are those respectively of a man, a lion, an eagle, and a bull (Plate 30).

Pursuing his fantastic ride, he reaches the *Sidrat el-Munteha,* the "lotus of extremity," where he sees a tree with emerald and pearl branches that flourishes on the right side of God's Throne (Plate 31). From its foot rise the sources of the Nile, the Euphrates, and two rivers of Paradise, the Selsebil and the Kawthar, whose water is whiter than milk and sweeter than honey. At this moment, three angels approach and offer the Prophet three cups containing milk, wine, and honey (Plate 32). Mahomet chooses the cup with milk and puts it to his lips. Seeing that he does not touch the other two, the angels praise his decision.

Having come this far, the angel Gabriel stands and says: "I can go no further," and, spreading his six hundred wings, he returns to the original form in which he was created (Plate 33), saying: "O Muhammad! approach as close as you can and prostrate yourself!" Going beyond the "lotus of extremity," the point at which the knowledge of earthly creatures ends, the Prophet bows down to the ground before the Throne of God (Plate 34), and with the eyes of his heart contemplates the Lord, seeing which, the angels cry out: "We bear witness that the Most-High is One and Living, that there is no other god but Him, and that Mahomet is His servant and messenger!" Here occurs the famous dialogue between the Almighty and his servant concerning the setting forth of the five daily prayers. The scene is generally described as follows. God says to Mahomet: "I impose fifty daily prayers upon you. Go and teach them to your believers!" Bowing before the divine will, he goes and on his way meets Moses, whom he tells of the order he has received from God (Plate 35). The Hebrew prophet, recalling the difficulties he encountered during his earthly life in leading the Hebrew people and on the strength of his experience, his knowledge of human nature and of the degree of piety among men, advises Mahomet to ask the Lord to lighten his obligation. Returning to the Throne of God, the Prophet begs the Almighty, who reduces the number of prayers by five. Mahomet comes to Moses again, who persuades him to ask the Eternal for a further reduction. The Lord, receiving his request favorably, lowers the number of daily prayers to forty. This still seems too many to Moses, and the Prophet goes back again to ask for a further reduction. Finally, after four more supplications, Mahomet is able to have the number of daily prayers set at five. Submitting to the divine Will, he hears the voice of the Lord say to him: "O Muhammad! I agree to give each of your followers who recites these five prayers in the ardor of his faith the recompense for fifty prayers; furthermore, the number of their good works and their fasts will be multiplied tenfold, and Paradise will be granted to them!"

Continuing his miraculous journey, the Prophet sees seven hundred thousand veils made of light, fire, hyacinth, pearls, and gold, each one guarded by seven divisions of angels (Plate 36). Having gone through them in succession, Mahomet sees the Throne of God, which is made of red hyacinth. A host of angels cricles around it singing litanies to the divine Name. Surrounding it are seven hundred thousand huge tents, each the size of the world, separated from each other by a space as great as a road fifty thousand years long, each tent occupied by fifty divisions of worshiping angels. On the point of reaching the Throne, the founder of Islam prepares to remove his sandals, but a voice is heard that stops him. Bowing down to the ground Mahomet, transported in a state of exaltation approaching annihilation, worships the Eternal (Plate 38). A *hadith* mentions that the Almighty then spoke ninety-nine thousand ineffable words to the Prophet and communicated to him the Law and various commandments intended for the Believers.

Leaving the Throne, the Prophet meets the angel Gabriel again. The latter has the new task of leading Mahomet through Paradise so that he may admire the place destined for the chosen. They go first to the Kawthar (Plate 39), created especially for the founder of Islam, whose water cures all thirst.

Its banks are bordered by domes of pearl, red hyacinth, and emerald. Coming to the gate of Paradise, they are welcomed by the angel at the door (Plate 40), who greets them and then brings them into a garden where a multitude of *houris* live. Birds perch on the heads of these marvellously beautiful women, some of whom are gathering flowers (Plate 41), while others are mounted on camels (Plate 42). They all seem extraordinarily happy and amuse themselves among garden plots filled with flowers. Approaching a palace, Mahomet recognizes one of the first women to embrace Islam, the second wife of Talha and mother of one of the Companions of the Prophet (Plate 43). The radiant look of the people who live in Paradise, their gaiety, their playful gestures, are a significant break with the hieratic attitude of the elect, the prophets and angels Mahomet has encountered in the heavenly spheres. Here mysticism is totally supplanted by a world in which material pleasures clearly predominate. We see as in filigree the evocation of a hospitable earth covered with gardens, crossed by streams of cool water, so longed-for by the nomadic, desert-dwelling Arabs. The elect in this paradise, more earthly than spiritual, are tall and about thirty years of age. They experience neither suffering nor desire, and are subject neither to old age nor to the necessities of nature. Each of them lives in a golden tent.

The Moslem conception of Paradise, in which the temporal element outweighs the spiritual ideal, has given rise to many comments and criticisms. The description of a fairy-land where the elect enjoy indescribable delights must certainly be considered as a metaphor whose meaning was clear to men of the desert, but which calls for transposition to an abstract and metaphysical plane. Nevertheless, going beyond such earthly perspectives, even as they may be interpreted by supernatural optics, certain mystics did not hesitate to affirm that the blessedness they sought above all was not based on sensual pleasures but was to be found only in ecstatic contemplation that leads to a fusion with God.

The first part of the marvellous journey is over; Mahomet under the archangel's guidance will now set off on the second part of his tour.

The tragic quality of the second part is present from the outset, when Mahomet comes to the gateway to Hell, where the enemies of the Most-High God are to be found. The angel Mâlik, prince of shadows, stands at the door. His aspect is terrifying. At the Prophet's request, he blows on the fires of Gehenna and they flare up terribly (Plate 44). At the center, a gigantic tree called *zekkum* fills a space as great as a road five hundred years long. Its thorns are like spears; its fruit is shaped like the heads of demons, lions, scorpions, and other hideous beasts, and is bitterer than poison (Plate 45). At the foot of the tree, the damned are tormented by demons who cut out their tongues, which immediately grow back. Gabriel explains to Mahomet that these wretches preached sobriety and abstention from all perverse acts during their lives, but in private gave themselves up to passion and sensuality.

Further on, evil spirits are engaged in cutting up the flesh of the damned and forcing them to eat it (Plate 46). This is the punishment for scoffers and for those who spoke ill of Moslems.

Continuing their progress through the infernal abyss, the Prophet, guided by the angel, sees the punishment of those who, having been guilty of cupidity, are now immobilized by their own monstrously distended stomachs (Plate 47).

Other sinners who, out of self-interest, brought false accusations to oppressors, spread discord among Moslems and used violence to seize their goods, are pierced with spears by red demons (Plate 48). Further on, the damned, half-naked and hanging from hooks over the infernal brazier, pay for the hypocritically pious and virtuous comportment they adopted on earth for the sake of temporal advantage. They are watched over by a fire-breathing demon (Plate 49).

Mahomet next sees the suffering reserved for women who let their hair be seen by strangers and, by an immodest attitude, led men into temptation. They are hanging by their hair in the midst of the flames, guarded by a black demon (Plate 50). Other women, bound hand and foot, are bitten by snakes and scorpions. Some, who insulted their husbands and went out of the house without permission, are hanging by their tongues over the flames (Plate 51); they are being punished also for having embarrassed their husbands by engaging in shameful acts.

Continuing his tour of the infernal regions, the Prophet sees the punishment reserved for those who stole the inheritance of orphans. Demons pour a poisoned brew into their mouths, which flows throughout their bodies and then passes out again (Plate 52). Further on, adulterous women hang from hooks through their breasts (Plate 53). They are also paying for the crime of having brought their illegitimate children under the familial roof in order to secure a portion of the husband's inheritance. Nearby, misers who refused to pay the tithe are sitting with heavy millstones fixed around their necks (Plate 54). The hypocrites and flatterers, their faces blackened, have chains locked around their necks and wrists and their feet in shackles. The Prophet then comes to the false witnesses: each of them is decked out with a pig's head and the tail and hooves of an ass. A hook comes out of each one's mouth, and they stretch out long tongues in an effort to cool their parched throats (Plate 56, upper part). Others who performed no good acts in their life are by turns killed and brought back to life again (Plate 56, lower part). Drinkers of wine who died impenitent are kneeling in chains, tormented by demons who pour an endless stream of poison into their mouths (Plate 57). Finally, the proud, locked up in boxes surrounded by fire, are tormented by snakes and scorpions (Plate 58).

In this Moslem Hell—an apocalyptic vision of shadowy realms intercut by spheres of fire where the condemned undergo a diversity of punishment in relation to misdeeds perpetrated during their earthly life—the damned, in sharp contrast to Believers, are hypocrites whose behavior and apparent good works concealed their lack of faith. Such an attitude was profoundly contrary to Moslem spirituality, sincerity and purity of intention being the essential bases of the religious and moral conceptions of Islam.

The Theme of Mystical Ascension

Stories of miraculous ascensions to the highest heavenly spheres are commonplace not only in the great religious traditions but among many spiritual traditions in which they have often served as a basis for mystical speculations.

The theme is already to be found in the Bible, where a famous passage from Genesis tells of the miraculous beginning of Jacob's journey into Mesopotamia: while resting one night after sunset, Jacob saw, as if in a dream, a ladder whose foot rested on the earth and whose top reached to Heaven, with angels going up and down on it. From on high, the Eternal spoke to Jacob, promising to protect him and to bless his posterity. The symbolic ladder, establishing a connection between cosmic regions, is found in traditional Moslem accounts of the *Mirâj*, which often show Mahomet climbing the steps of a luminous ladder rising up from the Temple of Jerusalem (or, more exactly, from the stone of Isaac) to Heaven.

The guide, frequently portrayed as a winged creature who points out the road to the mystical traveller and helps him along the way, is found in a number of accounts, notably in shamanic texts in which ascension by means of flight is considered a supernatural power, symbolized by a gigantic bird. In the Altaic and Turkish world, a general belief attributed to horses the power of flying up into the sky. In the 13th century, the grand shaman of Genghis Khan was reputed to have mounted into the sky on a grey horse. In India as well, the ability to fly through the air and cross immeasurable distances with the speed of lightning counts among the magic powers attributed to *arhat* in Hinduism and Buddhism.

Mazdaism also possesses, in its religious literature, the story (known as the *Ardâ Vîrâf Nâmeh,* most probably written down at the beginning of the second millenium of our era) of the miraculous journey of a certain Ardâ Vîrâf (5th or 6th century), undertaken in the role of messenger for his coreligionaries. It is made clear in the description of the meeting in the Temple of Fire that this holy man was charged with questioning the elect to see if they accepted or refuted the law observed by the followers of Zoroaster. Having taken a narcotic, Ardâ Vîrâf slept in the temple. For seven days and nights, guided by Serosh (protector of just souls) and by the Ized Atar (a divinization of fire), he came, first, to the *Chivenad poul* (a bridge from earth to Heaven), then to the various heavenly places, whose paradisal joys correspond to the degrees of virtue among the elect. In the second part of his journey, he is led through four infernal spheres, where he witnesses the sufferings inflicted on the condemned, whose punishments correspond to the various crimes they perpetrated during their earthly existence. In the last chapter of the work, Ardâ Vîrâf is brought before Ahura-Mazda, who declares to him that the only true Way is that of the purity and faith of Zoroaster's law.

The theme also appears in Christian literature, inspired not only by accounts given by mystics and visionaries but also by scenes narrated in cathedral sculptures and frescoes, which show by turns the blessings enjoyed by the saved in the heavenly realms and the sufferings reserved for the damned in Hell. Among texts of Christian inspiration, the one closest to the Moslem story is, by all evidence, the famous epic poem composed at the beginning of the 14th century by Dante Alighieri. In the *Divine Comedy,* we see the Tuscan poet undertaking his long journey through the world of souls, Hell and Purgatory first, where the Latin poet Virgil is his guide, then across the threshold to Paradise, where he continues his ascent under the guidance of his beloved Beatrice. Going through the different realms, he meets souls whose state of blessedness corresponds to the life they led on earth. The Dantean trilogy reaches its apotheosis when the poet is finally admitted into ecstatic contemplation of the divine Essence, veiled by the hierarchies of an angelic host that surrounds the throne of God.

The many analogies between them have led to the notion that the *Divine Comedy* was directly influenced by the *Mirâj Nâmeh*.[4] It is possible that the Florentine poet knew the Moslem work from Latin translations. In fact, in 1264, some decades before the composition of Dante's poem, a French and Latin translation was made by Bonaventure of Siena from a Spanish version, itself taken from the Arabic. A copy of this version has been preserved in the Bibliothèque Nationale.[5] Another, entitled *Liber scale Machemeti*, has been preserved in the Vatican Library.[6] Apart from the existence of these translations, the many references to the *Mirâj* in writings of the time allow us to think that Dante may at any rate have had some knowledge of Moslem eschatology. It is worth recalling that at this same time a number of scientific works that the Arabs had borrowed from the Greeks were translated into Western languages.

The depiction of the destiny of souls, and of the punishment of those who were guilty of grave sins during their earthly lives, also frequently appears in far-eastern manuscripts, of which the most well-known are the various versions of the *Sutra of the Ten Kings*, written in Chinese or Japanese on long illuminated scrolls which portray the judgments handed down by the kings of the ten infernal courts and the many tortures reserved for sinners.[7] Eschatology, which has a place in every civilization, has always been the great moralizing factor in religions and ideologies, despite the marked differences among them.

The Development of Eastern Art

ORIGINS

Marked off by oases where important religious, historical or artistic centers flourished, the great caravan routes crossing Central Asia were not only the cradle of Eastern artistic production but also the privileged place where contacts and exchanges between the great nomadic and sedentary civilizations multiplied. At the time when the Greco-Roman world discovered Chinese silk, the Roman and Alexandrian geographers Marinus of Tyre (1st century) and Ptolemeus (2nd century) had noted the existence of an itinerary which, starting from Antioch, crossed the Euphrates, penetrated the Parthian empire (which would be incorporated into the Persian empire of the Sassanids in 224), reached the Indo-Scythian empire, followed the Pamir, passing through Kashgar, Kucha, and Kharashar, to come finally to the region of Tuen-huang in the Chinese province of Kansu. Though eclipsed from time to time, the more than two-thousand-year history of the Silk Route and the great paths of the caravans shows these roads of communication as a melting pot of the styles and artistic traditions of cultures extending from China to northern Iran, which had become a crossroads between Siberia and India on the one hand and the high Mongol steppes and the Bosphorus on the other.

When Ardeshir, founder of the Sassanid dynasty (226–651), proclaimed himself King of Kings, Persia, freeing herself from Hellenic domination, undertook the restoration of her national culture. At this time (when Zoroastrianism, the doctrine of ancient Iran, was the state religion), there appeared a new faith of universal aspiration, Manichaeism, which combined Zoroastrian dualism with Gnostic Christianity. The art of painting in Persia goes back to Mani (216–275), the founder of the new doctrine. The exceptional quality of his paintings is a fact of history, not of legend. A century after his death, a doctor of the Eastern Church, Saint Ephram of Edessa (306–373), mentioned the existence of scrolls bearing pictures of angels and demons painted by the founder of the new religion. For his part, Saint Augustine (354–430) praised the beauty of Manichaean manuscripts with their skillful calligraphy and pictorial decorations.

THE MOSLEM CONQUEST

The almost constant struggle Sassanid Iran maintained over several centuries against the Romans, then against Byzantium, left the Persian empire exhausted at the very moment when the Moslem conquest began. Moved by a young but invincible faith, the Arab conquerors put an end to Iranian independence. From the 7th century, first in the name of Omayyad and then of Abbasid caliphs, Arab governors ruled the Iranian provinces. In 762 the capital was transferred from Damascus to Baghdad. This city, a center of religion and of the caravan trade, reached its apogee under Harun al-Rashid and remained a flourishing artistic center until its conquest by Turco-Mongol armies in 1258.

For many centuries Byzantium had exerted a local influence over the school of painting that grew up in Baghdad, the so-called Mesopotamian school, to which we owe the earliest known illuminated manuscripts.

THE DEVELOPMENT OF ISLAMIC ART

At the time when Baghdad was made capital of the Caliphs, Islamic tradition already condemned the portrayal of living beings. Moslem pictorial art (particularly in manuscripts) consisted mainly of frontispieces and chapter heads or *sarlohs* richly decorated with arabesques and interlacings of which gold and "lapis lazuli" blue form the essential elements. Made up of two types of ornamentation, the interpretation of floral forms and the use of geometric line-patterns, these motifs belong specifically to Moslem art. From the beginnings of Islam, painters and illuminators used this artistic technique in order to avoid the temptation to idolatry that might have come from the portrayal of animate beings. According to Koranic tradition, the reproduction of the human figure is a punishable act because it involves one in a creative activity that imitates Allah, the supreme Creator. It must be noted, further, that the face of the Prophet was rarely portrayed by Moslem artists, for the particular reason that he had received the Koranic revelations not only covered by a mantle, but with his face veiled, symbolizing the effacement of his personality before his prophetic mission. Nevertheless, this prescription with regard to the portrayal of animate beings—which was not specifically stated in the Koran—was far from strictly enforced.

The first Omayyad caliphs of Syria had already gone so far as to strike coins with human figures on them. If Islam never encouraged the portrayal of animate subjects, it still could not prevent figurative religious art from being created, particularly in Persian territory. Furthermore, there is no doubt that the non-Moslem conquerors favored the birth and development of the Mongol and Timurid styles, which produced masterworks among which the paintings illustrating the ascension and miraculous journey of the Prophet bear witness to a profound mystical inspiration.

Coming from a people without artistic tradition, the Moslem painters first looked to the work of those they had conquered, preserving, on the one hand, the great Sassanid themes or imitating Byzantine art, and on the other hand, receiving new artistic concepts from eastern Turkestan. Persian art, as a meeting point of distinct traditions, worked out a synthesis of many foreign influences and in this way created a new school, marked by the realistic character of its animate forms and by the typically ornamental aspect of its landscapes. If, in this new art, the most important trait of Sassanid origin is the portrayal of the fiery nimbus, the influence of Byzantium is visible particularly in the use of stylized shading and of a space in which voids are rare, and above all in the importance given to gold in the coloration. The use of gold in Eastern painting is ancient. The Manichaeans (whose art reflects that of the Sassanids) already used a quantity of gold and silver in illuminating their manuscripts.

From the first millenium of our era, alongside the Sassanid style, the influence of the pictorial art of Turkestan (particularly of the Turfan region) began to show itself, an art noted for the red or ochre-yellow tonality of its grounds and for the portrayal of landscapes after Central Asian models. At this time, Buddhism, which extended from China to eastern Iran, was an effective vehicle for Chinese influence, which had already appeared in paintings before the Mongol conquest.

THE MONGOL INVASIONS: SOURCE OF A NEW ART

Over the centuries, because of its geographic situation between the Mediterranean, Indo-Iranian and Chinese worlds, Upper Asia was a crossroads of great spiritual, artistic, and commercial currents moving between the West and the Far East. From the unification of Mongolia, carried out in the 13th century, came a powerful and remarkably well-organized empire. After his triumph over rival groups, Genghis Khan (1167–1227) was recognized as supreme Khan by the Mongols and their satellites. Having conquered China and taken Peking in 1215, the Mongols seized Bukhara and then Samarkand. Khanates were established in China, Turkestan, and Iran, putting an end to the caliphate of Baghdad. But this too-vast estate—covering an area from northern China to the Volga and from the edge of Siberia to India—rapidly broke apart, giving rise to three large empires, including that of the Timurids (1369–1500), which grew from the conquests of Timur Leng (1336–1405). Timur, a descendent of Genghis Khan, dreamed of reuniting Asia; having succeeded in a few years in subduing Persia (1389), he invaded southern Russia, seized Delhi (1397), took Syria from the Mamelukes (1400), destroyed Baghdad (1401), and attacked the Ottomans.[8]

If the Mongol invasions broke the artistic progress of the school of Baghdad, whose decline had set in with the taking of the capital of the Abbasid caliphs by the Il-Khans in 1258, the barbarian conquerors soon made themselves instruments of a civilization which they renewed with a brilliant admixture of Chinese influences. From that time, the reign of Timur, who had drawn all of Persia into his immense empire, opened one of the most remarkable epochs in the history of Iran and of Eastern painting. The Mongol pictorial style gave birth to three schools, located respectively in Shiraz, Tabriz, and Herât, where veritable academies made themselves guardians of certain artistic traditions.

The school of Shiraz,[9] capital of the province of Fars, mainly produced transitional works in which Iranian genius was able to preserve some aspects of traditional Sassanid art from the school of Baghdad. Its paintings are distinguished by the red or ochre-yellow tonality of the ground, and by elements borrowed from Central Asian models, particularly from paintings from Turfan and Turkestan. But Chinese influence is minimal.

The school of Tabriz,[10] located in the capital of the Irano-Mongol empire of the Il-Khans (1256–1353), was marked by considerable Chinese influence, due mainly to relations between the new masters of Persia and the Celestial Empire. Having become a capital, the city of Tabriz received famous Western travellers such as Odorico of Pordenone and Marco Polo. The school of illumination established there bore the imprint of a foreign inspiration, due particularly to the westward migration of a number of Chinese artists. In addition to this far-eastern influence, the school of Tabriz made significant innovations in the use of perspective. The pictorial art of China was progressively amalgamated with the ancient Iranian style, which finally succeeded in recovering its autonomy and in bringing about the rebirth of a typically national art.

But the greatest center of Timurid art in 15th century Iran was in Herât. The school bearing its name was born in the far-eastern province of Persia, and is the one that has passed down to us the greatest number of illuminated manuscripts. Also very much influenced by Chinese painting, the productions of this school reached a perfection that marks the zenith of the pictorial art of this time.

A Masterwork of Timurid Art[11]

The *Mirâj Nâmeh* in the Bibliothèque Nationale is certainly one of the greatest masterworks produced by the studios of Herât, the capital of Khurasan. Most probably executed by three different artists,[12] the sixty-one paintings[13] which decorate the manuscript, of great richness of coloration and infinitely delicate workmanship, clearly preserve the marks of the major artistic directions whose impulse goes back to the eminent bibliophile Bâysonqûr Mirzâ, son of Shah Rokh. For half a century, Shah Rokh (1396–1447), son and successor to Timur Leng, governed the region and made it the flower of a vast empire. Thinkers, poets, painters, and musicians contributed to the brilliance of his court. A great lover of manuscripts, he gathered a personal library which became widely renowned, and his royal studios housed calligraphers, illuminators, and bookbinders. Parallel to his artistic preoccupations, Shah Rokh made efforts to develop diplomatic and commercial relations with the countries of East Asia, thus creating artistic contacts with China, India, and Central Asia, as evidenced by the description of Buddhist frescoes in the records of his embassy in Peking (1419–1422), headed by Ghiyât al-Dîn at the request of the crown prince Bâysonqûr.

A synthesis of elements of various origin, the Timurid style of illumination of the school of Herât contains ancient traditional vestiges and characteristics that forecast the future development of the art of the Persian miniature. Analytic art, a mark of Moslem genius, is allied with Chinese influences characterized by the perfection of details. Deliberately abandoning the fresco in order to achieve compositions of a style close to perfection, the Timurid school acquired a new technique, that of the miniature, in which harmony of colors is combined with intensity of tones, in which the hieratic attitude of the figures is accentuated by elongation of the body, in which charming landscapes call to mind a fairy springtime, and in which the exterior architecture of sumptuous buildings, covered with arabesques, persists in ignoring perspective.

A typical expression of this artistic evolution, the *Mirâj Nâmeh* wins our admiration first by the great richness of its colors. The angel Gabriel spreads the multicolored fan of his wings with grace and variety in a sky filled with gold or silver stars. Timurid polychromy is particularly striking, not only in the representation of ceramics and faiences, but also in the fabrics of the clothing and wall coverings with their bright tonalities of violet, crimson, gold, indigo, yellow-gold, bright green, and in the luminous colors of the carpets. Each picture, dazzling the eye, looks like a stained glass window.

Along with the Prophet, the illuminations portray various figures from Biblical or Koranic tradition, as well as angels and demons. If the expression of emotion in these figures generally lacks spontaneity, by contrast their state of soul—by turns pensive, curious, withdrawn, majestic, admiring, resigned, sad, even savage—shows in the expression and direction of the pupils in their long, slanted eyes. The monotony of postures is broken, on the one hand, by the position of the heads, more or less inclined and often shown in three-quarter profile, and on the other by the gestures of the hands and the position of the long, slender bodies. Mahomet and the prophets who appear in the various heavens are all shown wearing beards, the beard being not only a symbol of virility and courage but also an ornament of the masculine face; properly trimmed, it was a sign of wisdom. The angels, who look like young women, have round faces, large dark eyes and arched eyebrows; their hair falls to their shoulders, except for two braids arranged in loops on top of the head in the Turfan fashion.[14] The manner of their portrayal goes back to Iranian pictorial tradition as exemplified by the Abbasid school. Another typically Iranian, or more precisely, Sassanid, characteristic appears in the fiery nimbuses that more or less completely surround the angels and holy figures. This motif—common in paintings from Chinese Turkestan dating before the year 1000[15]—was inherited from Mazdaism. It is depicted in the form of a flaming aureole and symbolizes the action of divine grace.

The clothing of the figure comes from Mongol tradition, characterized by a classical, almost impressionistic, style, with its long, generally one-colored robes, the sober folds drawn with fine lines, the crowns and hair styles of Timurid type. The feathers[16] that the *houris* and some of the angels wear in their hair also belong to Mongol dress. Among the Uighurs, ornithomorphic or feathered headdresses suggested the swiftness of bird-flight. Various accessories of dress[17]—belts and hats for example—are also rich in symbolism. Chinese historical writings state specifically that when the Uighurs presented themselves to the *Qaghan*, they would remove their hats and only salute him when their hair was hanging loose about their shoulders. Similarly, in the *Secret History of the Mongols*, an episode from the life of Genghis Khan relates that as an act of thanksgiving after an escape from danger, the emperor, holding his hat in his hand and having hung his belt around his neck, bowed down facing the sun.

Except for the *Burāq*, animal images are rare in the heavenly spheres. This extraordinary mount, who accompanies the Prophet in the course of his heavenly and infernal tours, is a fabulous and heavily symbolic animal. It has the body of a mule but the face of a woman, which the artists invariably show from the front. Topped by a Mongol crown, its long hair falls over a long arched neck. Its thick-set body and long, slender legs make it perfect example of the Iranian horse. It is noteworthy that, except for the position of the head and the direction of the eyes, the posture of the *Burāq* is often the same, which suggests that the artists who painted her made use of pumiced patterns.

Alongside the typically Timurid representation of the *Burāq*, the image of the cock (Plate 9) recalls in certain details the art of the animal painters of the school of Baghdad, to whom we owe, in illuminated copies of the *Fables* of Bidpay and the *Encyclopedia* of Zakariya ibn Muḥammad Qazvinî, many images of animals that are lifelike in form and realistic in appearance. The images of repulsive animals who take part in torturing the damned in Hell also recall, in their often unreal or apocalyptic character, certain aspects of the Abbasid school.

According to exegetic interpretations of a particular verse from the Koran, animals as well as men will experience resurrection and the last judgment, which may explain why Mahomet can behold camels and multicolored birds (Plates 41–42) in the gardens of Paradise.

The worlds through which the Prophet's nocturnal journey unfolds are portrayed in a manner that is typically Mongol. First of all, the indigo skies are enlivened by many tumultuous "Chinese" clouds, convoluted in form, with long tails floating behind them twining into garlands. This innovation is one of the most common for the representation of the firmament after the 14th century. However, the heavenly vault still kept, at that time, the little gold or silver discs (representing stars) inherited from the Mesopotamian school.

Seas and rivers are generally shown as expanses of dark water textured with many finely combed waves of gold and silver, meant to suggest the shimmering of water (Plates 6, 39). This ancient technique, found in Chinese painting, had also been used by Iranian artists since Sassanid times.

The representation of the gardens of Paradise (Plates 40–42) is more complex. The surface of the soil spreads out in wide bands, often broken down into longitudinal sections meant to simulate successive planes reaching to the horizon. These bands of earth are often covered with luxuriant vegetation. In this area the Timurid school was not far advanced, contenting itself with imitating old models of landscapes produced by Abbasid artists. The same is not true for the representation of trees: huge (Plate 31) or tall and slender (Plates 41–42), their trunks bear the stamp of far-eastern influence, which shows particularly in the drawing of the curved, flower-laden branches (Plates 41–42). However, these twisting trees, with their sinuous trunks and branches, are sometimes covered with a foliage of Abbasid style in which each leaf is distinctly drawn, depriving the ensemble of relief.

In the matter of architectural representations, Mongol art had progressed very little beyond the works of the Abbasid school, which are characterized by a total absence of spatial logic. Building exteriors are still flat in appearance (Plates 27, 39, 43). The absence of relief is accentuated by lack of the play of light and shadow necessary for suggesting depth. The steps of stairways, for instance, are clumsily interpreted (Plate 26). A few timid attempts at linear perspective, imperfectly realized, present us with buildings of a two-dimensional character and no suggestion of relief (Plate 23). If occasionally a sense of depth is discernible, it is due solely to the skilful disposition of motifs on successive planes (Plate 5).

On the other hand, these buildings or architectural forms, lacking chiaroscuro and so imperfectly depicted, attempt—by means of a richness, sometimes an excess, of decorative motifs, particularly elements of precious faience or polychrome enamel—to suggest majesty, even sumptuousness. Yet the costly draperies (Plates 36–37), the walls covered over with arabesques and interlacings (Plates 27, 39, 40), and the luxury of details do not succeed in making us forget the almost total absence of perspective. The same is true for the rare depiction of furnishings—carpets, floor lamps, a pulpit (*minbar*), thrones (Plates 2, 4, 5, 12, 26, 41)—which are also treated without modeling, in the Abbasid manner. Nevertheless, architecture occupies an important place in Timurid art; sometimes it is even portrayed in an impressive way, as for example in the depiction of the domes (Plate 39) over the gates of Paradise, where the richness of decoration, the polychrome enamels, the Kufic inscriptions above the doors, win our admiration.

The Making of the Manuscript[18]

In the royal workroom, once the composition of a manuscript was decided upon, the first task consisted in assembling the necessary materials for the scribes and illuminators. Among these materials, the most important were the paper, the inks, the brushes, and the various colors, including gold and silver.

The making of paper, which originated in China, was introduced into Moslem territory in 751. The Arabs learned the technique from Chinese prisoners they brought to Samarkand after the battle of Talas, fought in that year, had made them masters of Turkestan. The invention immediately took root in the city, where a workshop was opened in the second half of the 8th century. The industry reached Baghdad in 793, then in the course of the following centuries spread little by little to the various Mediterranean countries. The technique reached great perfection in Khurasan, where paper was made using linen fibers.

Once the studio had acquired the valuable paper, properly finished and sometimes lightly tinted, the first operation consisted in deciding the layout of the pages, that is, in determining the amount of space reserved respectively for the text and the illuminations, in order to achieve a harmony between facing pages. The relation between margins and written surface also had to be predetermined, as well as the number and placement of the lines, which were marked out in intaglio by pressing lightly on a silk thread attached to the edges of a sheet of cardboard and placed over the paper to be ruled.

The calligraphy generally preceded the execution of the paintings, which, however, had to be sketched out beforehand (it can be seen in certain places that some of the written characters are partially covered by paint). The ink used for the writing was made either from lamp-black mixed with honey or from a gallnut extraction. The titles and some passages (or words) of the text were often done in gold or silver ink or in various colors of paint. The copy would close with a final note, the colophon, in which the calligrapher would record, besides his name, the place where the work was done and the date of its completion. The sheets were then put in order, by means of catchwords, a system of Arab origin which consisted in writing on the lower margin of the verso of each page the first word on the recto of the following page.

Once the calligrapher had finished his work, the artists (there were often several) would begin the painting of the miniatures. From Timurid times on, there was a strict association between picture and text. Generally the drawings were done by great artists, guided by their own inspiration. For less important illustrations (or for transition scenes), the studio possessed collections of tracings of various subjects and decorative elements to use as models. The technique consisted in transferring the model to a piece of gazelle hide (or other transparent support); the artist (or his assistant) would then make a stencil by pricking out the outline of the model with a pointed tool. Placing the stencil over the sheet to be illustrated, he would then transfer the pattern with charcoal dust. The illuminations were executed with fine brushes and pigments (often very costly) of animal, vegetable, and mineral base. Certain metallic pigments could only be applied over protective coatings that would ensure adhesion to the paper and eliminate as far as possible the risks of corrosion. Sometimes the brightness or reflectivity of the golds or silvers was enhanced by drawing fine lines or dots over them with an ivory stylus. Once the painting was finished, the last operation consisted in smoothing the picture by placing it against a plank of polished chestnut and rubbing it with a crystal or agate ball. Unlike the calligraphers, the illuminators rarely signed their work.

* * *

A rare specimen of profoundly religious painting, in which inspiration has produced one of the most precious masterworks of Timurid art, the *Mirâj Nâmeh* is of exceptional interest in that, beyond telling the story of the Prophet's ascension, it recalls an historical event whose commemoration was fixed on an anniversary day (the 27th *radjab*) and celebrated, from the end of the 7th century, at the Dome of the Rock in Jerusalem, the third holy city of Islam.

The message contained in the account is of moral as well as doctrinal character; in fact, the text and illustrations in this manuscript bring out, alongside eternal truths, a sharp and vigorous censure of the morals of Mahomet's time. From a doctrinal point of view, this event of great spiritual importance—which from the earliest times was the basis for many stories—has given rise to discussions concerning the exact nature of the miraculous journey. Certain theologians have believed that the Prophet was actually carried off to Heaven, a phenomenon made possible by physical weightlessness due to Mahomet's holiness. Other doctors of theology have thought that only the soul of the founder of Islam, momentarily detached, was taken up to the seventh heaven and then sent back to earth to re-enter the Prophet's body. The mystics, far from seeking rational explanations, have been unanimous in their belief in the real ascension of Mahomet to the divine Throne, in the course of which he met the great prophets who preceded him in his mission.

However it was, the extraordinary account of this miraculous journey which marked the founder of Islam with the "Seal of the Prophets" and impressed generations of men with its supernatural ideality, counts among the spiritual treasures of humanity.

PLATES

AND

COMMENTARIES

PLEASE note that, since this is an Eastern manuscript, the pages in the original volume proceed from right to left, rather than the reverse, as in Western manuscripts. We have, therefore, followed this arrangement of pages, with Plate 2 falling on a right-hand page and Plate 3 facing it on a left-hand page. We have also respected this order on the Commentary pages, e. g., the Commentary for Plate 2 is on the right-hand page and the Commentary for Plate 3 on the left-hand page, facing each other and preceding the Color Plates they describe.

Plate 1

INITIAL SARLOH (f. 1 v°)

A magnificent *sarloh* painted in gold and colors in the style of Herât. Calligraphed in Uighur script among the elegant arabesques of the central motif is the title-line: "Thus did the Prophet (salvation be upon Him!) accomplish the *Mirâj*."

Among the traditional decorative motifs of Islamic illuminated manuscripts, the richly decorated frontispieces or *sarlohs* appear as one of the constants in an art which theological imperatives had rendered non-figurative. Often composed of interlacings and garlands of polychrome flowers set off against a gold or "lapis lazuli" blue ground, these precious decorative compositions reproduce or take their inspiration from the designs of early Oriental carpets; yet they are, at the same time, an aesthetic symbol representing the Garden spread with flowers, trees, and real, figurative or mystical motifs. In Islamic areas, the use of the *sajjāda* (prayer carpet) goes back to very distant origins. According to one legend, the angel Gabriel brought Adam a carpet made from the hide of a sheep from the gardens of Paradise. A true *templum*, the prayer carpet is a sacralized space isolating the one praying from the profane world. Originally made from palm leaves or the tanned hides of sheep or gazelles, the traditional rugs were later woven out of various textiles. The designs, influenced by the technique of weaving, had to form a point on one of the narrow sides. During prayer, the point was set in the direction of the Kaaba (at first the point, or "*qibla*," was aimed towards Jerusalem, but Mahomet, disappointed by the obstacles his preaching had encountered among the Jews, redirected the prayer toward the great religious center of Islam at Mecca). This point is often reproduced in the pictorial carpets or *sarlohs* placed at the beginning of illuminated manuscripts.

The technique of weaving, embroidering, or stitching inscriptions in gold thread on strips of silk or brocade was a source of inspiration for the miniaturists who, traditionally, gave over the first and sometimes the last leaves of manuscripts to these sumptuous ornaments in the midst of which the titles and occasionally the colophons were written out.

عن انس بن مالك رضي الله عنه عن النبي صلى الله عليه وسلم اتي بالبراق

Plate 3

ON THE WAY TO JERUSALEM (f. 5)

According to the legend, the Prophet would accomplish his "*Mirâj*" mounted on an extraordinary beast, the *Burāq*, traditionally portrayed as resembling a mare or a mule, but with a woman's face, the tail and feet of a camel, with a harness of pearls, a saddle made of emerald (or some other precious stone), and stirrups of turquoise.

At the beginning of the fantastic ride through the heavenly spheres, peopled with angels whose multicolored wings rainbow the sky, Michael, one of the archangels of Islam, bearing a standard (a symbol of protection which already makes a link between the heavenly and earthly spheres) and with Gabriel at his side, leads the Prophet to the Mosque at Jerusalem.

This particular version says that Mahomet presented himself "before the holy House and entered into the al-Aksa Mosque." An historical clarification is called for. If over the centuries Jerusalem has been a sacred city for Moslems, one explanation of that fact is that the Prophet departed on his miraculous ascension from a spot located precisely within the enclosure of the Temple of the Sacred City. It should be noted, however, that the magnificent Mosque of the Dome (or Dome of the Rock), which replaced a provisional sanctuary built by the Calif Omar (581?–644), was constructed on the grounds of the ancient Temple of Jerusalem by the Calif Abd al-Mâlik at the end of the 7th century. This monument (incorrectly called the Mosque of Omar) stands on the exact place from which, according to Moslem tradition, Mahomet was taken up to Heaven. The al-Aksa Mosque, situated at the southeast end of the Temple enclosure, was built slightly later, at the beginning of the 8th century.

Plate 2

THE ANGEL GABRIEL APPEARS TO THE PROPHET (f. 3 v°)

In the initial vision preceding the Prophet's ascension, the angel Gabriel presents himself to Mahomet and tells him that God, filling him with His bounty, has decreed that in the course of the night he will be raised up to the seventh Heaven and permitted to look upon the work of the Almighty and to worship the face of the Eternal. "God commands you," says the angel, "to come before His Majesty. The door to the Seven Heavens is open and the angels are waiting for you. Rise up, O Envoy of God, and let us go!"

The angel Gabriel, the most popular in Moslem angelology, is, with Michael, Azrael, and Israfel, one of the four archangels of Islam. His essential function consists in transmitting God's orders to the Prophets; it was from him that Mahomet received the Koranic revelation. If his name appears only three times in the Koran, he is nevertheless mentioned many times under other appelations. His legend as God's messenger is sometimes mixed with certain biblical stories, above all with accounts of two apparitions found in the New Testament, one to Zacharias (Luke 1:11–20), the other to the Virgin Mary (Luke 1:26–37).

Here, the Prophet—prior to being transported to the "distant Mosque"—is shown inside his house near the sacred Mosque at Mecca. The angel, with multicolored wings, is kneeling at his feet. Mahomet, surrounded by a fiery nimbus, is portrayed lying down; the thoughtful and majestic gaze of his long, slanted eyes rests on the angel. The interior of the house is suggested by a window-door, carpets, draperies and rich fabrics, and ceramic tiles. This painting shows clearly the two-dimensional character of pictorial composition in early Timurid art, in which the artist renounces the interpretation of volume. However, luminosity of color, purity of line, and subtlety of decoration make up for the ignorance of perspective, the lack of foreshortening in the carpets and floor-tiles, as well as for the absence of chiaroscuro.

9 ... الله صلی الله علیه وسلم براغه بنوب ملائکلر صاغنده و صولنده خدمتنده طوروب سنجاق آلنده حاضر اولدقلری محلدر

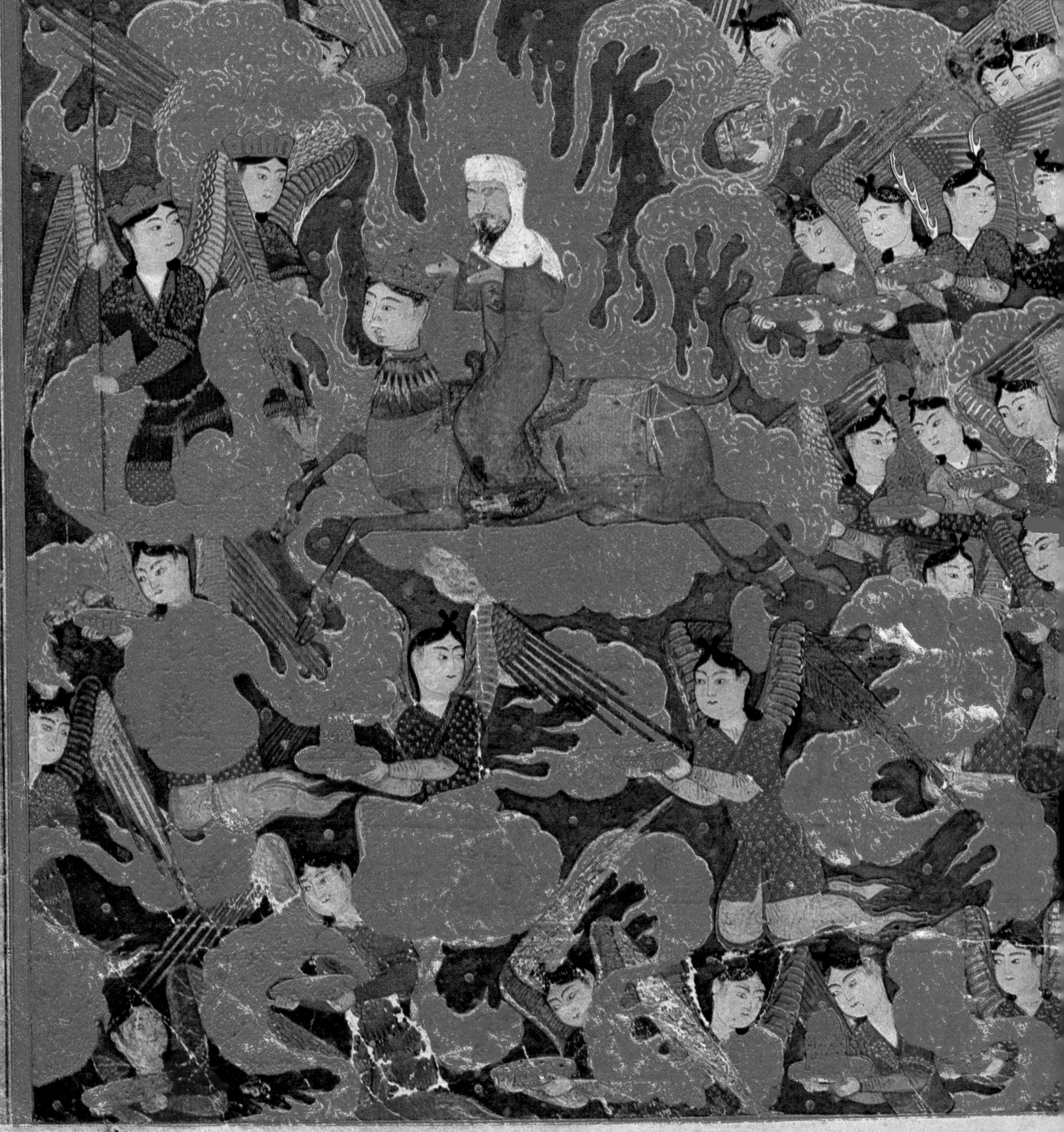

مجيء جبرئيل عليه السلام واخباره للنبي صلى الله عليه وسلم انّ هذه الليلة ليلة المعراج وانّ الله تعالى يطلبك

جبرائیل علیه السلام رسول الله صلی الله علیه وسلامه کلوب بو کیجه لیلة المعراج در حق تعالی سنی حضور شریفنه دعوت ایلدی کوکلار قپوسی آچلوب جمله ملائکلر سنکا منتظر درلر

جبرائیل علیه السلام رسول الله صلی الله علیه وسلم حضرتلرینه کلوب بو کیجه لیلة المعراج در حق تعالی سنی حضور شریفنه دعوت ایلدی قات کوکلار قپوسی آچیلوب جمله ملائکه سنکا منتظرلردر قالق کدلوم یا رسول الله دیدیکی محلدر

Plate 5

THE PRAYER (f. 7)

The archangel Gabriel having given the call to prayer, Abraham asks the Prophet Mahomet to serve as *imâm*. The term *imâm* refers to one who stands in front of the faithful to direct the canonic prayer and indicate the ritual acts that must be performed by the assembly. In the beginning, the *imâm* was the Prophet himself, perhaps as he is shown in this painting. After calling down blessings on the faithful, he raises his hands toward the sky, a gesture immediately repeated by the prophets, who cry out "*Amîn*!"

In the mosque are seven figures shown in the half-kneeling, half-sitting position, usually known as *djulus*, that comes between two prostrations. In the center, Mahomet, seated on a *sajjada* (a prayer carpet on which the *qibla* can be seen, pointing in the direction of the holy place), is enveloped in a flaming aureole. To his left are three prophets wearing traditional turbans; to his right the three other figures veiled and dressed in brown. Seven lamps hang from the arches of the painted ceiling, forming an ornamental frieze across the upper margin. The lamps and lanterns are part of the customary furnishings of a mosque, along with the carpets which, besides their use in the *salat*, also lend beauty to the sacred building. Sumptuous carpets are hung at the back of the oratory here. The structure of this composition is exceptionally interesting because of its success in imitating Far-Eastern techniques of perspective in which the disposition of figures on successive, superimposed planes gives the impression of three-dimensionality. The floor tiles are again treated flatly, but by contrast the prayer carpet has been drawn with a serious attempt at foreshortening—a new element in Timurid art.

Plate 4

MAHOMET ENTERS THE SACRED MOSQUE AT JERUSALEM (f. 5 v°)

Accompanied by the archangels Michael and Gabriel, Mahomet enters the sacred Mosque at Jerusalem, where he meets the prophets who preceded him. Several come forward to meet him, among them Ibrahim (Abraham), Musa (Moses), and Isa (Jesus). Having greeted him, they say: "Rejoice, for the Most-High has filled you with His bounty. This night, all that you ask of the Lord, He will grant you."

The building, shown here, in which this first meeting takes place, is recognizably a mosque—probably the one built in Jerusalem on the very spot from which, according to Moslem tradition, Mahomet was taken up to Heaven, or else the later al-Aksa Mosque situated at the southeast end of the Temple enclosure. The text makes it clear, but the picture also shows, by a lamp hanging from the ceiling, that the building is a mosque. The architecture retains the characteristics of an old style; columns support the arches of the ceiling; the corner-stones are decorated with polychrome floral paintings. The carpets and tiles show no foreshortening; the six human figures and two angels are placed on the same horizontal plane, doing away with any illusion of perspective. But brilliance of color compensates for the structural weaknesses of this monumental ensemble. The Prophet is shown standing, entirely enveloped in the prophetic flame, dressed in the jade green tunic he will wear throughout the journey. Hands tucked into his sleeves in a hieratic attitude, he turns his slanted eyes with their dark pupils toward the group of fellow prophets come to meet him. Two of these figures are wearing turbans, the other three a brown veil, the *taylasan* formerly worn by the *cadis*. All are enveloped in the prophetic aureole.

ه النبي في بيت المقدس وامامته للانبياء المذكورين عليهم الصلوة والسـ
حضرت رسول عليه السلم بيت المقدس ده ذکر اولغان انبيايه امامت اندوکی حال ده صلوات
الله عليهم اجمعين

سول النبي صلى الله عليه وسلم ورويته لابراهيم وموسى وعيسى عليهم ال

Plate 7

TO THE FIRST HEAVEN (f. 9)

Riding the *Burāq* with its mauve trappings, and guided by the archangel bearing a standard, the Prophet Mahomet proceeds toward the first Heaven, where he will be greeted by twenty divisions of angels. The story tells us that this first sphere is the color of turquoise. In several places, the Koran (LXVII, 3; XXIII, 88; XLI, 11) mentions the seven Heavens of Islam in which God's messengers traditionally dwell. Generally, Adam is placed in the first Heaven, John and Jesus in the second, Joseph in the third, Idris in the fourth, Aaron in the fifth, Moses in the sixth, and Abraham in the seventh. Paradise itself is also in the seventh Heaven. However, the Uighur version of the story bears notable variants in its designation of the Prophets who dwell in the various spheres.

Throughout his miraculous tour, Mahomet is shown wearing a white turban, his head surrounded by a nimbus of high flames rising from his shoulders. This Sassanid motif, sometimes confused with the crescent moon, gives a divine character to supernatural beings, whose images had become classical in Central Asia, Tibet, and on the borders of China. The flaming nimbus, inherited from Mazdaism, was specifically meant to represent *far*, the action of divine grace. More generally, an elliptical aureole around the head (sometimes around the whole body) suggests spiritual light received and reflected, the sacred brightness. It is at the same time a materialization of the aura, a luminous cloud emanating from certain exceptional beings.

Plate 6

ON THE SHORES OF THE KAWTHAR (f. 7 v°)

Having left Jerusalem, preceded by the angel Gabriel and mounted on the *Burāq*, the Prophet rides up into the sky and arrives at the shores of an immense sea suspended in air by effect of divine power and of which only the Eternal knows the full extent. In many places the Koran mentions the Kawthar as well as the four Rivers of Paradise (the River of Water, the River of Milk which does not deteriorate, the River of Wine, and the River of Clarified Honey) which flow into it. The generations that came after the Prophet pictured this sea surrounded by banks of gold and resting on a bed of rubies and pearls. Already in the Bible the Promised Land, Canaan, had been described as a land flowing with milk and honey.

Here, the Kawthar is shown as a wide and very dark body of water textured with many finely combed waves of gold and silver (unfortunately tarnished by age) which originally must have given it a shimmering effect. Winging over this sea, the *Burāq* seems to fly in a sky scattered with "Chinese" clouds. Its young woman's face is shown in three-quarter profile on an arched neck; its short body, regularly shown from the side, rests on long, slender legs. Portrayed in this way, it recalls not only the ancient Iranian motif of the winged horse, but also the favorite animal of Mongol painting, a horse galloping with easy grace.

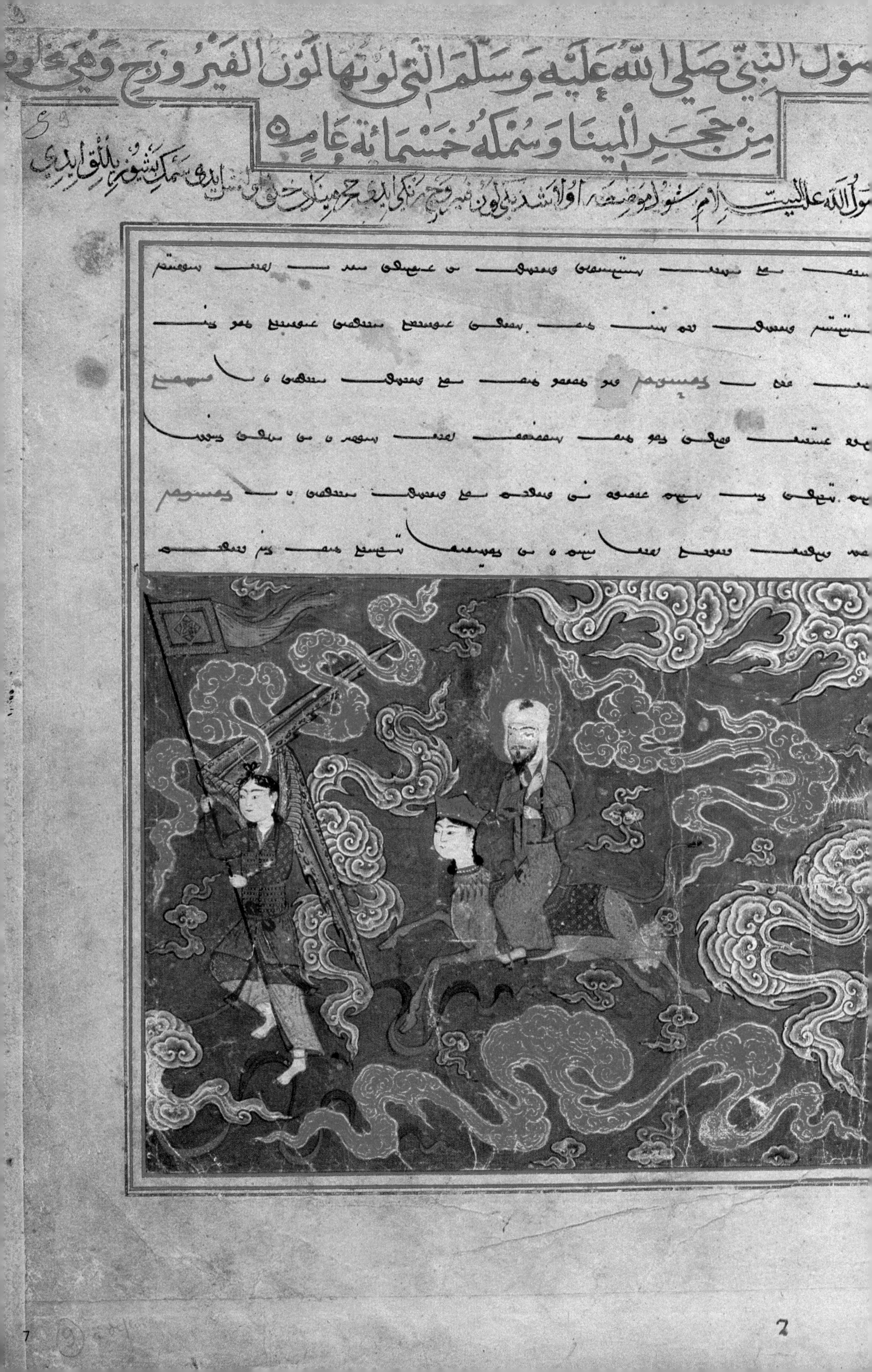

سول النبي صلى الله عليه وسلم التي لونها لون الفيروزج وهي ...

من حجر المينا وسمكه خمسمائة عام

...صلى الله عليه وسلم من بيت المقدس ورؤيته للسلم الذي حول الس...

...يته للبحر الأسود الذي يسمى بالكوثر وهو واقف في الهوا...

رسول الله صلعم بيت مقدسدين چيقب اطراف سماده نردبان كوروب ودخي بحر اسود كوروب آدنه كوثر ديرلر هواده معلق طورر ايدي

Plate 9

THE PROPHET COMES TO THE WHITE COCK (f. 11)

Continuing on his ride through the first Heaven, Mahomet, accompanied by the angel Gabriel, sees a White Cock whose comb grazes the foot of God's Throne and whose feet rest on the earth. Gabriel, in answer to the Prophet's question, explains that this cock is an angel in charge of counting the hours of the day and night. When the hour for prayer comes, he beats his wings, so large that they cover the heavens and the earth, and gives his crow, which is an act of faith: "There is no God but Allah!" Hearing him, all the roosters on earth, in turn, sing the praises of the Eternal.

Familiar in its realism, this image of the Cock takes from the Mesopotamian school (to which we owe several pictorial versions of the Fables of Bidpay) its lifelike appearance and the precision of its outline. Carried away by a desire to make a realistic representation of the bird, the artist who painted this particular picture forgot to take account of the Moslem tradition which says that the Cock's wings should be decorated with emeralds and pearls.

This image of the angel-cock suggests certain sources, particularly shamanistic sources, according to which angelic creatures are able to fly because they are ornithomorphic. Mentioned in the *Avesta*, the cock, a sun-bird, seems equally connected with the cult of Mithra, in which it is a symbol of resurrection and eternal life. For the first time since the beginning of the fantastic ride, the sky (always covered by the famous "Chinese" clouds) is embellished with stars, represented in the form of large drops of gold of the type found in paintings from the School of Baghdad.

Plate 8

MAHOMET MEETS THE PROPHET ADAM
(f. 9 v°)

Having arrived at the first Heaven, always led by the angel Gabriel and mounted on the *Burāq*, Mahomet is welcomed by the angel at the door who expresses his joy at the meeting. He then sees the Prophet Adam who, after greeting his "son" and wishing him peace, shows a surprising behavior. The legend tells us that he appears happy looking to his right, and smiles; but looking to his left he turns grave and weeps. Gabriel explains to Mahomet that on his right Adam sees the souls of the saints, the prophets and the chosen, and looking on them his heart is made glad; but on his left he sees the souls of the unfaithful, the wayward and the unbelievers, and is covered in sorrow. According to Moslem tradition, Adam's repentance was accepted by God, but nevertheless his original disobedience was punished by exclusion from the Earthly Paradise, which thereafter became for the first man and his descendants the goal which they might reach once again by their own efforts.

The Koran, in many places, evokes Adam as father of the human race, the chosen one of God, before whom, by divine order, the angels had to prostrate themselves, and to whom God had shown all the generations of men and their prophets. According to certain traditions, man as the Almighty created him, although guilty of concupiscence, was given reason in order to triumph over it, and by that fact his nature is higher than that of the angels.

Adam, first of the prophets, stamped with majesty, is shown here standing, his turbaned head surrounded by a flaming nimbus (a legend relates that after the exile from the Earthly Paradise, the angel Gabriel wound a turban around Adam's head in memory of his lost dignity).

... از النبي صلى الله عليه وسلم ... في الأرض ورأسه تحت العرش

11

رسول الله عليه السلام سمايه اوليه واصل اولدقده عرشدين بر آق خوروز كوردي كه باشي عرش آلتنده ايا قلاري ير يوزنده باصلمش اول محلده

...النبي في السماء الأولى لآدم صلوات الله تعالى عليهما وسلا...

حضرت رسالتنگ معراجنده اوّلکی کوکده آدم پیغامبر غم بولشوب سلام دیردکن حضرت آدم علیکم السلام یا ابنی الصالح یا نبی الصالح دیوب عزّتله سلامنی آلدی حلد...

Plate 11

ARRIVAL AT THE SECOND HEAVEN MADE OF WHITE PEARLS (f. 13)

Coming to the second Heaven, which is as wide as a road five hundred years long, Mahomet, mounted on the *Burāq* and preceded by the angel Gabriel, finds himself in the presence of twenty divisions of angels ready to serve him. Gabriel looks at them and points back to the Prophet, who is surrounded by an immense flaming aureole. The angels stand in ranks before the new arrivals, their hands crossed in the attitude of slaves in the presence of their master.

The eight angels here, who represent the twenty divisions mentioned in the text, wear their hair in the Turfan fashion, long at the nape of the neck, with small braids at the ears and two more braids arranged in loops at the top of the head. As in the preceding pictures, they are portrayed with feminine features. This custom among Timurid painters may reveal the influence of an old polytheistic tradition, rejected by the Koran, according to which the angels were Allah's daughters. It is to Timurid iconography that we owe the gold Mongol crown worn by Gabriel and the *Burāq* and the rich polychrome decor of the sky full of Chinese clouds and garlands.

Plate 10

THE ANGEL HALF-FIRE HALF-SNOW (f. 11 v°)

Before they leave the first Heaven, Gabriel brings Mahomet to an angel made half of fire and half of snow. When he recites the *tesbih,* his voice is so resounding that it sounds like thunder. In his left hand he holds a rosary of snow, in his right a rosary of fire. This religious object is composed of three groups of beads, each separated by two larger beads. Traditionally, the number of beads should add up to a hundred, a symbolic number arrived at by enumerating the ninety-nine names of the divine attributes, reflecting an intense metaphysical exaltation (among the qualities attributed to the Eternal are such names as "the Merciful," "the King," "the Powerful," "the Creator," "the Omnipresent," "the Light"), and adding to them the name of Allah. The texts tell us that the sound of thunder comes from the moving of the beads during the recital of these invocations. Near the angel stands angelic troops who call upon the Eternal, imploring Him, saying: "O God, Thou hast brought snow and fire together. In the same way let all Thy servants be united in the faith of obedience to Thy law."

The dualism suggested by the two constitutive elements of the angel shown in this picture is a reminder that, according to Hebraic and Islamic texts, the angels were created by God half of water and half of fire. It should also be noted that the Syrian Apocalypse of Baruch (XXXI, 6) states that they were made of fire and flame, and that the Book of Enoch mentions angels made of snow, hail, heat, and cold.

٧

19

صول النبي صلى الله عليه وسلم الى السماء الثانية التي هي مخلوقة من
من اللؤلؤ الأبيض ٥

رسول الله صلى الله عليه وسلم ایکنجی قات کوکه کیدکی محلدرکم آق لولودن یرادلمش ایدی

120

رؤية النبي صلى الله عليه وسلم للملك الذي نصفه من الثلج ونصفه من النا

في يده الواحدة سبحة من النار وفي الأخرى من الثلج والرعد صوت تسبيح ذلك الم

رسول الله عم اوّلکی وایکنجی سما اورتاسنده بر ملک کوردی نصفی قاردن ونصفی آتشدن برالنده قاردن تسبیح وبر آلنده ناردن کوک کورلدکی اول تسبیحک صداسیدر

[illegible]

[illegible]

[illegible]

[illegible]

[illegible]

[illegible]

[illegible]

[illegible]

[illegible]

Plate 13

THE ANGEL OF PRAYER (f. 15, upper part)

Moving through the second Heaven, guided by the archangel, the Prophet, mounted on the *Burāq*, sees an extraordinary angel with seventy heads, each of his heads, according to the text, having seventy tongues, and each tongue speaking seventy forms of praise in honor of the Most-High. The role of worshipping angels and of the praises they address to the Eternal has an important place in the Koran, notably in *sura* XL, 7 ff., where the "prayers of the angels" are discussed.

The fantastic image of this many-headed angel (the heads built up in a reverse pyramid, starting from the principal face of the figure) has an apocalyptic, almost agonizing, resonance. It also suggests innumerable Buddhist icons, notably Avalokitesvara of the eleven heads and the thousand eyes, which were common in India, Tibet, and Central Asia during the 8th–11th centuries. Many mythologies speak of polycephalic beings, in whom the numerical symbol is combined with various aspects of their manifestation.

Plate 13

MAHOMET MEETS THE PROPHETS JOHN AND ZACHARIAS (f. 15, lower part)

Before leaving the second Heaven, Mahomet, preceded by Gabriel and riding his special mule, sees two figures who greet him. The angel informs him that they are Yahia (John) and Zakaria (Zacharias). Having greeted him, they cry out: "O Muhammad, welcome; your presence honors the heavenly world. May the bounty of the Most-High be yours!" These two prophets are often mentioned in the Koran, which counts Zacharias among the number of just men and relates in particular the miraculous birth of his son John (*suras* III, 33–36, and XIX, 1 ff.), speaking of the latter's wisdom but omitting mention of his role as the Baptist and of his tragic end, though certain later Arab writers, notably al-Tabari (9th–10th century) and al-Masudi (10th century) give the full story in various places.

The biblical prophets, wearing white turbans, their heads surrounded by the prophetic flame, stand upright in a quasi-hieratic attitude. The angel Gabriel seems to be making introductions. The sky is filled with stars (in the form of gold drops) and Timurid clouds.

Plate 12

MAHOMET MEETS THE ANGEL OF DEATH
(f. 13 v°)

In the second Heaven, the Prophet, under Gabriel's guidance and riding his unusual mare, comes first to a gigantic angel whose mission is to decide the lot of all creatures. Clearly he is Azrael, one of the great angelic figures, of whom it is said that his feet are on the confines of the earth and his head is in the highest Heaven, and that he has a chair of light on which he rests one foot while the other stands on the bridge between Paradise and Hell.

Islamic dogma accords a very important place to angelic beings. God has placed four archangels at their head: Gabriel, messenger of Allah; Michael, who watches over the natural world; Israfel, who will sound the trumpet of the Last Judgment; and Azrael, angel of death.

The angel personified in this illumination, of imposing size, is seated on a sort of golden throne (note that, traditionally, only the seat of honor on which the sovereign sat was elevated), wearing a headdress of blue and gilt feathers. This ornithomorphic headdress appears for the first time in the present manuscript. The feather, an ornament of Mongol origin, begins to figure in iconography in the 13th century, and it is interesting to recall that, among the Uighurs, ornithomorhpic headdresses were meant to suggest the swiftness of birds.

...سول النبي صلى الله عليه وسلم الى الملك الذي يعين ارزاق جميع المخلوقات

رسول الله صلى الله عليه وسلم سماء ثانيده جميع مخلوقاتك رزقلرين تعيين ايدن ملكه واصل اولد...

[illegible]

[illegible]

[illegible]

[illegible]

[illegible]

Plate 15

ON THE THRESHOLD OF THE THIRD HEAVEN, MAHOMET IS WELCOMED BY A HOST OF ANGELS (f. 17)

Mounted on the *Burāq*, and led by Gabriel who is surrounded by a flaming nimbus, Mahomet reaches a new heavenly sphere made of red hyacinth. The angel guarding the door says to the Prophet: "O Muhammad! be honored for the bounty of the Most-High!" Thirty divisions of archangels are there, with more than 30,000 angels ready to obey each of them. They all greet the Prophet.

Timurid iconography generally liked to represent angels dressed in short-sleeved vests, slipped over long one-piece robes with long sleeves (sometimes so long that they hang down and totally conceal the hands). Calm folds, drawn sometimes with light and fine lines, sometimes heavily, give their outlines a hieratic appearance. They are shown wearing gold crowns of the Mongol type, their hair dressed in the manner frequently adopted in Central Asia. They wear belts made of pearls, or of long ribbons whose curls and loose ends are drawn out into garlands that overlap with the patterns of the Chinese clouds.

Plate 14

TO THE THIRD HEAVEN (f. 15 v°)

Leaving the second Heaven, guided by the angel Gabriel, Mahomet continues on his ride in the direction of the third Heaven. The text tells us that at this point he sees a White Sea, but the painter has not included it in his picture.

From an iconographic point of view, the transition scenes illustrating the passage from one Heaven to the next (cf. especially Plates 6, 15, 24) are very much alike. Only certain variations—in the direction of the faces, the position of the hands, above all in the more or less majestic deployment of the angel's multicolored wings and the variety of fabrics in the clothing—provide, through richness of color, an impressionist or a classical character that breaks up the monotony of these scenes of passage.

It is interesting to note how often the *Burāq* is drawn in the same posture; its feet especially are shown in exactly the same fashion. This fact suggests that the artists who drew the *Burāq* made use of stencils, having only to retouch the head because its position varies with each scene. Furthermore, in the same way, the outline of the Prophet (except for his head and hands) is shown many times in exactly the same posture.

النبي صلى الله عليه وسلم الى السماء الثالثة

وصول النبي صلى الله عليه وسلم الى البحر الابيض الذي في نواحيه ملائكة كث

حضرت رسالت پناه عليه السلام آق دكزن وار دب اطرافنده جوق ملايكه وار ايدي اول محا

Plate 17

MAHOMET BEFORE THE PROPHETS DAVID AND SOLOMON (f. 19)

Leaving Jacob and Joseph behind, Mahomet, always preceded by the angel Gabriel, glimpses two other figures: David the Prophet-King, and his son, the Prophet Solomon. In many places, the Koran evokes the legend of the Prophet-King, which was elaborated on by such eminent Arab authors as al-Tabari and al-Masudi. As for "Suleiman ben Dawud" (Solomon son of David), Moselm legend makes of him a personality of the first order; Arab historians consider him a leader of the people, more glorious even than Alexander the Great; his marvelous magical and divinatory powers, his skill in rendering justice, his esoteric learning—he knew the language of birds and other animals, storms obeyed him, he commanded the djinns (this power is often suggested in the magnificent frontispieces in illuminated versions of the *Shâh-nâmeh*)—are particularly noted, and the Koran designates him as a veritable apostle of Allah.

The pictorial execution of this scene is very much like the preceding one. Each figure has the same posture; only the faces, the position of the hands, and the arrangement of the angel's wings give variation to the composition. As in the preceding picture and in almost all representations of the prophets, the figures here are wearing turbans, the headdress adopted by Moslems consisting of a band of material wound around a cap. In Islam, the turban is a symbol (national, religious, even professional) of dignity and power, and often is the distinctive sign of a Moslem as opposed to an infidel. Its most common color is white, generally considered one of the colors of Paradise.

Plate 16

THE PROPHET MEETS JACOB AND JOSEPH
(f. 17 v°)

Continuing on his way across the third Heaven, Mahomet, his body entirely surrounded by the prophetic fire, preceded by the archangel, comes before two figures encircled by fiery nimbuses, one with a face "as round as the full moon." Gabriel immediately introduces them: "These are the Prophets Yaqub (Jacob) and Yusuf (Joseph)." Having greeted Mahomet, they wish him welcome. These two biblical figures occupy an important place in the Koran, where Jacob is counted among the prophets. To the biblical legend, the sacred text of Islam adds an account of the extraordinary psychic bond between Jacob and his son Joseph, notably in the episode in which a wolf frightens Jacob instead of Joseph (XII, 13) and then when Joseph's coat is sent to Jacob, who identifies it from far off by its perfume, thanks to which he recovers his sight (XII, 93). As for Joseph (cf. *sura* XII, which is devoted to him), he is the symbol of the just man who succeeds in keeping to the straight path and is able to forgive his enemies. His is one of the favorite legends in Islam. The same *sura* XII tells his story at length, involving prophets, angels, the devil, djinns, men, and animals.

The figures shown here are typical of the Timurid manner of portraying man. All have long, slanted eyes which, indicating direction with their dark pupils, throw out lively, sidelong glances. The heads are in three-quarter profile. The adults have oval faces, beards, and moustaches; the angel (Gabriel), the adolescent (Joseph), and the *Burāq* have round faces.

ؤيته صلى الله عليه وسلم لداود وسليمان عليهما السلام

ول الله صلى الله عليه وسلم داود پيغمبر و سليمان پيغامبر عليهما السلام ايله مصاحبت اتدكاري مقام در

وانْ مِنْ هُنَاكَ وَرُؤْيَتِهِ لِيَعْقُوبَ وَيُوسُفَ عَلَيْهِمُ الصَّلوٰةُ وَالسَّـ

حضرت رسول علیه السلام اوچنچ قات کوکدا یعقوب پیغامبر علیه السلام و یوسف پیغامبر علیه السلام نی کوردوکی مقام شریف

Plate 19

ARRIVAL AT THE FOURTH HEAVEN (f. 22)

Having crossed the threshold of the fourth Heaven, always guided by Gabriel, Mahomet, surrounded by the prophetic nimbus, continues on his ride and comes to a group of angels whose only function is to praise God. They welcome him and stand in his presence, hands crossed, as slaves stand before their master. According to Moslem tradition, God granted to angels the possibility of taking on human form; the same tradition tells us that prayer is their food and holiness or purity their drink.

A number of times (Plates 11, 16, 20, 23, 30, 34, 39), the angels are shown bareheaded. In many Oriental civilizations, certain accessories of dress, such as hats or belts, have a symbolic significance. In that light, it is interesting to note that in coming into the presence of the sovereign, the Uighurs would take off their hats and let their hair fall loose about their shoulders. This group of angels seems then to be welcoming the Prophet as a sovereign. [Following this picture there is a lacuna in the manuscript which deprives us of illuminations showing the figures Mahomet meets in the fourth Heaven. The absence of at least one page is confirmed by the catch-word written at the bottom of f. 22 v, which does not correspond to the first word on the next page.]

Plate 18

THE ANGEL WITH SEVENTY HEADS (f. 19 v°)

Before leaving the third Heaven, the angel Gabriel brings Mahomet before an angel with seventy heads, each head having seventy tongues with which it recites seventy forms of praise.

The number seven, in Islam, is rich in symbolic meaning, which seems to go back to borrowings not only from the Jews and Christians but also from pre-Islamic Arab culture. It seems above all to be considered a whole, a festive number, the symbol of perfection. The number "seven" appears many times not only in Moslem tradition but in the text of the *Mirâj Nâmeḥ*: the miraculous journey of the Prophet unfolds, in the first part, through the seven Heavens, which Mahomet enters by going through seven doors; then it moves to Hell, described in Moslem tradition as composed of seven infernal spheres. The iconography of the present manuscript also underscores the symbolism of this number—and of its derivatives or multiples—with its implicit idea of totality and universality.

ول النبي صلى الله عليه وسلم إلى السماء الخامسة التي هي مخلوقة من الذهب

رسول الله عليه السلام التنجي فات كوككه كجدكي تحلدكه حق تعالى صافي آلتوندن خلق ايتمش ايدى اول محلدا

ؤية النبي صلى الله عليه وسلم في جنب بحر كبير ملكا كبيرا بسبعين رأس

رسول الله علیه السلام دریا کنارینده یتمش باشلو براولو ملک کوردکی مجلس

Plate 21

ARRIVAL AT THE SIXTH HEAVEN (f. 24)

Guided by the angel Gabriel, the Prophet, surrounded by a prophetic nimbus and riding the *Burāq*, comes to the sixth Heaven. The angel guarding the door greets Mahomet and calls down divine blessings on him. Sixty divisions of angels stand beside him reciting litanies.

According to Koranic tradition, the seven Heavens are peopled with angels in various forms occupied with glorifying God in all tongues and without interruption. The sound of their voices is like thunder. Already in the Bible, the angels were described as servants of God whose first duty was to praise Him. The Book of Enoch mentions myriads of angels who stand before the Eternal and celebrate Him in alternating choirs. The cosmological superposition of the heavenly spheres allows for determining a hierarchy among celestial beings according to the Heaven each occupies. Together they make a court around the Eternal and praise Him; however, certain ones are sent out as messengers to men, while others stand to the right and left of each human being and report on all his actions, good and bad.

Plate 20

IN THE FIFTH HEAVEN, WITH THE PROPHETS ISHMAEL, ISAAC, AARON AND LOT

(f. 22 v°, upper part)

Riding the *Burāq* and preceded by the archangel, Mahomet comes to the fifth Heaven, made of gold, where he meets four great prophets: Ishmael and Isaac, sons of the patriarch Abraham; Aaron, who was spokesman for Moses; and Lot, the prophet who opposed vice and was thereby a model for Mahomet. Having greeted the founder of Islam, who is surrounded by a flaming nimbus, they say to him: "O Muhammad! all that you ask of God, this night, He will grant you. Ask of Him salvation for the souls of those who submit to your Law." Note that in Islam, God gave the prophets the task of imposing total submission on believers.

In many pictures, the *Burāq*, crossing the immensity of the heavens, seems to fly, its feet resting on nothing but the vault of the sky, always filled with clouds and stars. In the Altaic world and in old Turkish beliefs, there was a general conviction that horses were capable of flight and therefore of ascending into the heavens. In China as well, mystical journeys were well known many centuries before the Christian era; witness the legend according to which Lieh-tzu had the power to ride on the wind (undeniably a mark of great holiness), and the famous passage from the *Chuang-tzu* in which Kwang Ch'eng-tzu, teacher of the Yellow Emperor, declared to his illustrious pupil that he would lead him "to the summit of Light" and "to the doorway of Shadows." This theme of a miraculous ascension is in fact common in iconography of Taoist inspiration, in which the immortals are transported through the clouds on the backs of cranes or flying dragons.

Plate 20

ON THE SHORES OF THE SEA OF FIRE

(f. 22 v°, lower part)

Moving on, the angel Gabriel leads the Prophet, on his mule, to the shore of a Sea of Fire. The angel points to it and says: "On the day of resurrection, this Sea of Fire will be poured down into Hell and the damned will be tormented by it."

According to the traditional Moslem description, Gehenna consists of seven flaming regions, concentric and superimposed. Souls must cross a bridge over it, which the holy do easily, the just in a shorter or longer time; but the impious, unable to cross, plunge into the abyss. At the end of the world, it is said that God will open a pit of fire that will consume everything. Hell is mentioned more than fifty times in the Koran, but always somewhat laconically; most often it is evoked in an architectural image, occasionally in the conception of an animal.

ل النبي صلى الله عليه وسلم الى السماء السادسة التي خلقت من اللولو

22

١٢

عليه السلام سمای خامسه‌ده وصول بولوب ایدی سمای سادسه کیم لولودن مخلوق ایدی اول حالده
یدینچی قات کوک

ؤيته لأسمعيل واسحق ولوط عليهم الصلوة والسلام ورؤيته للبحر ا

ن النار وقول جبرئل عليه السلام انه يصب به في جهنم يوم الق

رسول علیه السلام اسمعیل و اسحاق علیه السلام و لوط علیهم کوروب ... نی یاردن بردگنی کوروب جبرئیل علیه السلام خبر بردی کیم قیامت کونیده بو دگنی جهنم دوکولور دیدی کی مخلددر

Plate 23

MOSES (f. 26)

The great biblical prophet, shown here surrounded by a prophetic nimbus, occupies an important place in the Koran, where Mahomet considers him his own precursor and model. In fact, they had many points in common, particularly that they both received .revelations and became preachers of monotheism. Moses is shown standing before a palace. The story tells us that the Hebrew prophet laments because until the coming of Mahomet he thought he had reached the most eminent rank, but now he understands that Mahomet surpasses him by far and that his followers are less numerous than those of the founder of Islam. At this point, the Eternal speaks to Moses, reminding him that He had made him illustrious among all men by speaking with him face to face and by delivering him from his enemies. He points out, further, that Moses should be offering acts of appreciation for the gifts he received from the Almighty.

In various places many figures from the Old Testament appear, not only in the *Mirâj Nâmeh* but in the text of the Koran itself. In effect, in order to illustrate the guiding ideas of Islamic doctrine, the Prophet borrowed certain stories from ancient biblical tradition because they were well known to his contemporaries.

Plate 22

APPROACHING MOSES (f. 24 v°)

Continuing on his ride, Mahomet, guided by the archangel, glimpses Moses, the great Hebrew prophet, on the way ahead. The various versions of the *Mirâj Nâmeh* locate in each of the seven heavenly spheres the residence not only of the great prophets of Islam but also of a number of important figures from the Bible. According to Moslem dogma, while the ordinary dead must wait in their graves for the last judgment, the prophets and martyrs go directly to Paradise—which explains why traditional accounts of the miraculous ascent of the founder of Islam mention meetings with Adam, John and Jesus, Joseph, Idris, Aaron, Moses, and Abraham.

The Prophet's face has been erased from this painting, most probably by a Moslem faithful to Islamic tradition, which never encouraged the depiction of religious scenes. In fact, the Koran sets down no prohibition with regard to figurative painting. The ban came solely from tradition. But it raised religious scruples to such a point that certain great artists, notably a celebrated painter from Baghdad who was one of the pioneers of Timurid art, did not hesitate in their old age to destroy all of their works which were contrary to the Moslem tradition with regard to figurative painting.

...ويه النبي صلى الله عليه وسلم لموسى عليه السلام وبكاء موسى عليه ال...

فلما فارقه رسول الله صلى الله عليه وسلم ومضى سمع موسى خطاب الح...

رسول اكرم عليه السلام موسى پيغامبر عليه السلامي كوردي جميع انبيادن هر بر فرد رجا ايلدكى مآب عاليه...

اول بر صحيفه يه [illegible] رجا ايدوب

[illegible]

[illegible]

[illegible]

[illegible]

[illegible]

[illegible]

[illegible]

Plate 25

TO THE SEVENTH HEAVEN MADE OF LIGHT (f. 28)

Led by the archangel, Mahomet, mounted on the *Burāq*, comes finally to the seventh Heaven, made of light, the dwelling place of seventy divisions of archangels put under the protection of the angel who guards the door to this heavenly sphere. Gabriel has had to address the angel guarding the entrance to each of the successive Heavens they have reached. Islamic tradition holds that God created angels of different forms and dimensions to serve different purposes. Their activity extends particularly to watching over the doors to the Heavens which they must protect against the assaults and curiosity of djinns and demons. The Koran relates that any djinn or demon who attempts to approach one of these doors will instantly be stoned or struck down by a falling star (XXXVII, 7 ff, and LXXII, 8).

The different versions of the *Mirâj Nâmeh* present notable variants with regard to the composition of the seven Heavens. Generally, the first Heaven is said to be made of iron, the second of copper or bronze, the third of silver, the fourth of gold, the fifth of a precious white pearl, the sixth of emerald, and the seventh of ruby or topaz.

In Islamic tradition, light (of which the seventh Heaven is made in this version) is a symbol of divinity. The Koran (XIV, 35) declares: "Allah is the light of the heavens and the earth. . . . God leads who He will to His light. . . ." According to certain mystical texts, "God is the one Light from which all lights proceed."

Plate 24

MAHOMET COMES BEFORE THE PROPHETS NOAH AND IDRIS (f. 26 v°)

The angel Gabriel next leads Mahomet, enveloped in the prophetic flame, before Noah and Idris, whose heads are encircled by fiery nimbuses.

The great events that marked out the life of Nuh (Noah) are often mentioned in the Koran. A mortal like any other mortal, he was sent among the unbelievers; as prophet, he announced and preached monotheism; but not received by his own people, treated as an impostor or one possessed, he was followed only by the lowly. Nevertheless, because of his faith, the Lord, when he sent the flood, allowed Noah to escape the cataclysm.

As for Idris, he is only mentioned twice in the Koran. His name was long an enigma. Certain Moslem writers identified him as Enoch (immortalized in legend) and accorded to this pious man a life of 365 years, making him a solar hero. Furthermore, legend presented him as a sage, inventor of the *qalam* and of cloth clothing. His title of "prophet" was due to revelations he received from the angel Gabriel; he was given the name "Idris" because of his knowledge of ancient revelations.

وصول رسول الله صلى الله عليه وسلم الى السماء السابعه

رسول الله علیه السلام یدنجی فلککه واصل اولدقدن براق ایله نوره غرق اولدقلری مقام شریفدر

رؤية النبي صلى الله عليه وسلم لنوح وادريس عليهما الصلوة وا

رسول الله عليه السلام نوح عليه السلام و ادريس عليه السلام ايله بولشوب مصاحبت ايدكلري حالدر

Plate 27

THE GOOD AND BAD MOSLEMS (f. 30)

A little further on, the Prophet finds himself facing two groups of Moslems. The first group is composed of men wearing white tunics; those in the second group wear white tunics striped with black. The angel Gabriel, addressing the first group, permits them to enter the palace with their Prophet and follow him wherever he goes, but he will not let the other group enter. Here we see Mahomet inside the palace accompanied by the good Moslems, while the bad Moslems remain outside.

These white or black-and-white tunics emphasize the hieratic appearance of the figures. From the Mongol period on, such long, plain robes were drawn with a number of long folds, giving them a severe look. Throughout his tour, Mahomet wears a white turban of the old style (wound around a cap) and the legendary green tunic belted at the waist. In Islamic tradition, the color green has good portents; the mystics believed it to symbolize peace and divine grace. But for the Moslem, green is not only the emblem of salvation (the Islamic flag is green) but also the symbol of the highest temporal and spiritual values. Certain texts recall that the Prophet's daughter Fatima, with her husband and children, sought refuge under the patriarch's green mantle in a time of danger.

Plate 26

ABRAHAM (f. 28 v°)

Mounted on his strange mule and guided by Gabriel, Mahomet comes up to a large palace. Leaning against it is an emerald-green throne, and seated on the throne he sees a figure with a white beard. Gabriel informs him that this patriarch is his ancestor Ibrahim (Abraham). Having greeted the newcomer, Abraham says: "O Prophet of prophets, welcome! God bless your arrival!" Gabriel (shown here encircled by a fiery nimbus) says, pointing to the palace: "This is your home and that of all who follow your way. Go in and explore it, for each day seventy thousand angels come to visit this house."

Mahomet's supreme model, Abraham, the man chosen of God, is one of the greatest prophets of Islam. He is, furthermore, the acknowledged ancestor of the three monotheistic religions, Judaism, Christianity, and Islam, and thus their spiritual link. Chosen by God to lead men to the worship of the one true God, he was the first to fight against polytheism. He founded the Kaaba where he prayed with his son Ishmael for a prophet to be sent down to Mecca, and he showed total obedience and an unconquerable faith in the tragic episode involving the sacrifice of his son to the Eternal. Islamic tradition relates that during one of his journeys to Hidjaz, the patriarch Abraham received from God a stone of immaculate whiteness which, with Ishmael's help, he set into a wall that he built with his own hands. Around this sacred Stone a pilgrimage was instituted, and it was on this blessed spot that the sacred city of Mecca was constructed.

...ية النبي صلى الله عليه وسلم لفريقين احدهما البسهم ابيض والآخر ملمع و...
...ه وجبرائيل اذن لهم ان يجوا معه في هذا المقام الشريف ولم ياذن لأصحاب الشا...

30

رسول الله عليه السلام سماء سابعه ده ايكي بولوك طائفه كوردي بر بولوك آق كيرديم (لباس) دير بولوك الاجه لباس كيرمش جبرائيل عليه السلام آق لباس كيكنلره اجازت ويردي رسول الله بله بجه‌ديلر الاجه كيكن طائفه‌يه اجازت ويرمدي الله اعلم

ية النبي صلى الله عليه وسلم لابراهيم عليه السلام فوق منبر من زبرج

رسول عليه السلام ابراهيم پيغمبر عليه السلامني كورديكي زبرجددن منبر اوزرينده خطاب ايدر اول عالم شريف نبوي

Plate 29

BEFORE THE ANGEL WITH SEVENTY HEADS (f. 32)

Continuing on his way, Mahomet, riding the *Burāq* and guided by the angel Gabriel (both are encircled by fiery nimbuses), comes before an angel of colossal proportions who has seventy heads. Each of his heads has seventy tongues which praise God night and day, reciting litanies of the names of the Most-High. Next to him stands another immense angel from whose eyes pour the waters of all seas, in an attempt to join the one world to the other.

In the Koran, Allah is qualified by a series of epithets, "His most beautiful Names," ninety-nine in number. Their enumeration, in litanies, is uttered by the multitudes of angelic beings. According to a prophetic *hadith*, "God has ninety-nine names, one hundred minus one. He who knows them will go to Paradise." These praiseful epithets, which name abstract and descriptive qualities (meditating on them enables the Believer to reach the highest spiritual truths), have nevertheless often been considered the expression of an anthropomorphic view of God. This notion has caused and still causes heated debates around the unity of the divine Essence. More than a century before the elaboration of these litanies by the Sufis (8th century), the Buddhists had composed laudatory enumerations of the names of Buddha in texts known as the *Buddhanama*, which were recited daily in the religious services of certain sects.

Plate 28

ON THE SHORES OF THE BLACK SEA (f. 30 v°)

The angel then leads the Prophet to a Black Sea, in which Mahomet, entirely surrounded by the prophetic flame, sees a numberless host of angels. Questioned about the blackness of this sea, Gabriel answers that only the Most-High knows the nature of it. On the bank stands a gigantic angel whose head grazes the foot of the divine Throne and whose feet rest on the ground. His mouth is large enough to swallow all the seven levels of the earth. His function consists in praying to God, begging him to pardon the sins of Believers.

The angels in this picture (as in other pictures in the manuscript) are shown with ears that have elongated earlobes, a feature characteristic of Buddhist art, which traditionally portrays the figure of Buddha with very long earlobes, in recollection of the heavy princely earrings worn by the young Siddartha Gautama (the future Buddha) during the years that he spent in the palace of his father, the king Suddhodana.

ه صلى الله عليه وسلم ملكا بسبعين راس وطوله بمقدار الدنيا وفي كل راس
سبعين لسانا يسبح الله تعالى بكل لسان ورآى ملكا اخر ان صب جميع البحار في عينه
لا تلحق الى عينه الاخرى

به النبي صلى الله وسلم عليه لبحر اسود وفيه ملائكة كثيرة وسواله عز جب
البحر وقول جبريل ان هذا البحر لا يعلمه الا الله تعالى وراى النبي في جنب
البحر ملكا راسه تحت العرش ورجله على الارض

Plate 31

AT THE FOOT OF THE TREE WITH EMERALD BRANCHES (f. 34)

Moving further on, they come to the *Sidrat el-munteha*, the "lotus of limit" (Koran LIII, 14), where the Prophet sees a great tree with branches of emerald and pearl, laden with fruit of all kinds and of exquisite flavor. From the foot of the tree spring four rivers, two above ground, two below. Of the first two, one is the Nile which flows through Egypt (Misr), the other the Euphrates, whose course passes through the city of Kufa. Of the two subterranean rivers, one is the Selsebil that flows into Paradise, the other empties into the Kawthar.

In this image of a tree we find a characteristic feature of Iranian mythology, in which the tree, generally shown beside a spring, symbolizes creation. But the image suggests above all the passage from Genesis (II, 9–10) which describes the tree of life, planted in the middle of Paradise, and encircled by a river divided into four branches.

Plate 30

THE ANGEL WITH TEN THOUSAND WINGS AND THE FOUR-HEADED ANGEL (f. 32 v°)

Further on, Mahomet, mounted on the *Burāq* and accompanied by the angel Gabriel, sees an angel with ten thousand wings standing almost over his head in the Black Sea. He dives down and comes back up shaking his wings, and, through the creative power of God, each drop that falls from his wings becomes an angel. This metaphorical figure was no doubt inspired by a belief according to which God sent Gabriel each day to the Garden of Eden where he would dip his wings in a river and shake them off, and from each wing would fall seventy thousand drops which turned into angels. Next to him, upright, stands an angel with four heads: of a man, a lion, an eagle, and a bull. According to Islamic belief, the bearers of the divine Throne appear in the four forms of a man and a bull (who intercede in favor of men and beasts of burden), an eagle and a lion (interceding for birds and wild animals).

This symbolic figure suggests Ezekiel's vision, while he was living with the captives exiled in Babylon (ca. 593 B.C.) beside the river Shobar, of four living creatures with the faces of a man, a lion, a bull, and an eagle. These images, expressing a totality, were also emblems of the four cardinal constellations of the zodiac.

ول النبي صلى الله عليه وسلم الى شجرة سدرة المنتهى ورآها شجرة عظيمة بعض اغص
برجد وبعضها من اللؤلؤ واوراقها كآذان الفيل وثمراتها كثيرة ويخرج من
اربعة انهار

Plate 33

THE ANGEL GABRIEL RETURNS TO HIS ORIGINAL FORM (f. 36)

Gabriel arrives and says to Mahomet (who is entirely enveloped in the prophetic flame), "I can go no further." And having alighted, he returns to his original form, spreading his six hundred wings to east and west. They have, in fact, reached the point beyond which Mahomet will have to abandon the *Burāq*; it is the *Moqam Zaribet* that he is about to enter, the place destined for the closest friends of God, and he will have to go there alone.

According to certain writers, Mahomet once asked the angel Gabriel to reveal himself in his true form, the one he takes in Heaven. Gabriel said that the Prophet would be unable to stand such a vision. But Mahomet having insisted, the angel appeared to him descending from the Arafat Mountains, filling all space from the east to the west. His head touched the heavens, his feet rested on the earth, and the colors of his wings were of a blinding brightness.

Plate 32

THE THREE CUPS MADE OF LIGHT (f. 34 v°)

At this point three kneeling angels present Mahomet, surrounded by the prophetic flame and mounted on the *Burāq*, with three cups made of light. In one there is milk, in the second wine, and in the third honey. Mahomet takes the one containing milk and puts it to his lips. Seeing that he does not touch the others, the angels congratulate him, saying: "You have done well to choose the milk and drink it, for all who follow your way, avoiding error, will depart from the world with their faith."

In certain versions, the honey is replaced by water, which has led some commentators to conclude that if the Prophet had chosen either water or wine, the choice would have foreshadowed shipwreck or waywardness for his followers.

عضار الملائكة لأجل النبي صلى الله عليه وسلم ثلاثة أقداح الواحد لبن والآ
الاخر عسل وشرب النبي قدح اللبن لا غير فقال له الملائكة نعم ما فعلت يا محمد
اللبن وحده ولم تشرب غيره فان امتك يخرجون من الدنيا بالايمان وفرح بهذا

رسول الله عليه السلام اچون اوچ ملائكه ... ... كطوروب اللارينده اوردن اوچ قدح بيري سوت وكيريسي شراب وكيريسي عسل الديلر ... سوت

غيريسنه ديمه دي
جبرائيل ايدي رسول الله
تحسين الدوروب ايدي
داوردك شراب ايچمادك
احمدك اگر ايچسه ايدنك
امتنك ضلالة دوشردي
ديدي ...

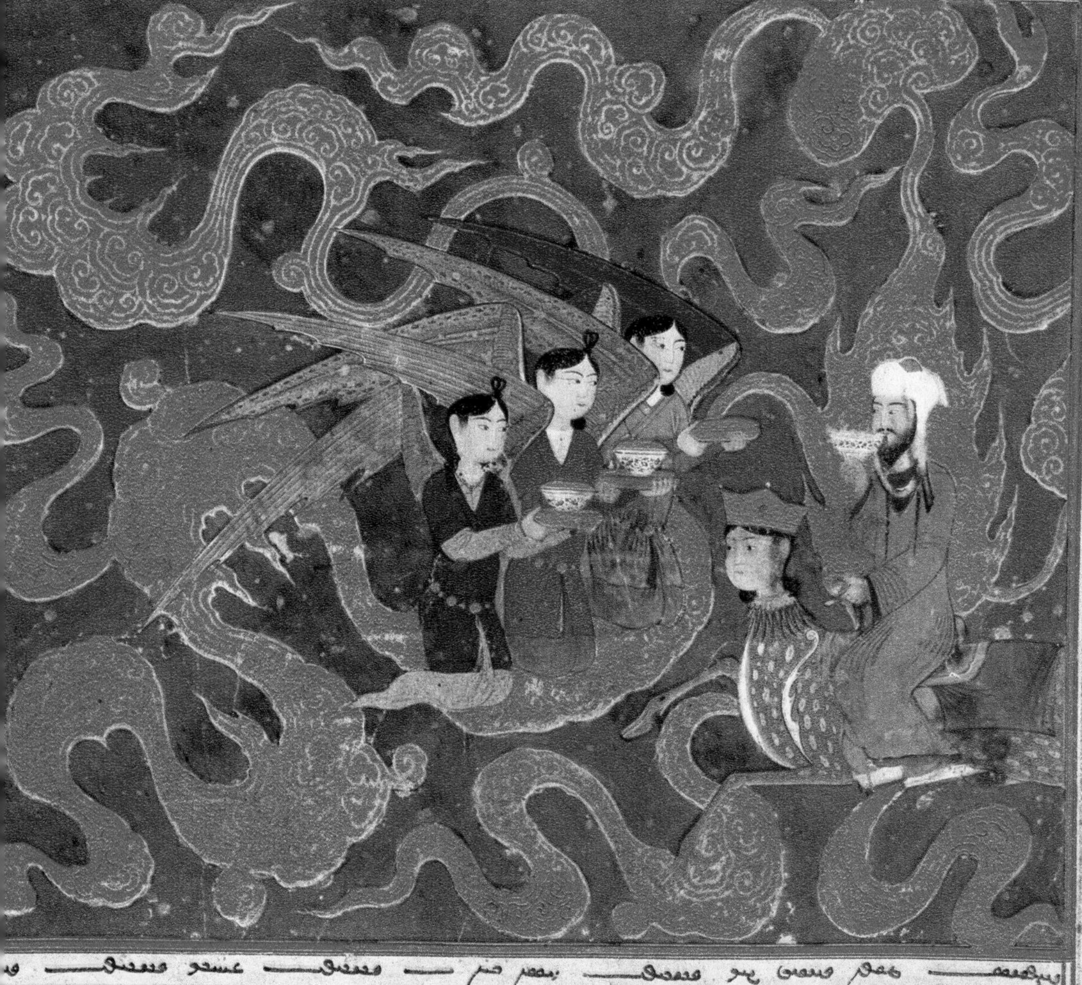

Plate 34A

CALLIGRAPHY PAGE (f. 38)

Plate 34

MAHOMET BOWS DOWN TO WORSHIP THE ETERNAL (f. 36 v°)

Coming to the place of worship, Mahomet bows down to the earth (or, here, to the clouds in the blue and gold sky), and cries out: "My heart has felt the Majesty of God and my eyes have looked upon It!" The Eternal then says to him: "Lift up your head and glorify My name!" The angels, seeing the Prophet so close to the divine Majesty, proclaim: "We bear witness that the Most-High Lord is One and Living, that there is no other God but Him; we witness, further, that Mahomet is his servant and envoy." This formula, which has a sacred value—it is the profession of faith (*shahada*) and of spiritual adherence to Islam—is one of the five pillars of the Moslem religion, the other four being the daily prayer, the ritual alms-giving (*zakat*), the yearly fast of Ramadan, and the pilgrimage to the holy city of Mecca.

The Prophet is shown here entirely enveloped in that golden flame that radiates from his body and that seems to serve as support as he bows down in the blue and gold sky.

[illegible] التحيات لله والصلوات والطيبات

[illegible]

[illegible]

[illegible] السلام عليك ايها النبي ورحمة الله وبركاته

[illegible]

[illegible] السلام علينا وعلى عباد

الله الصالحين [illegible]

[illegible]

[illegible]

[illegible] اشهد ان لا اله الا الله واشهد ان محمدا عبده ورسوله

[illegible]

[illegible]

[illegible]

[illegible]

[illegible]

[illegible]

[illegible]

سول النبي صلى الله عليه وسلم الى مقام القربة واشارة جبريل انه مقام
ال الله اسجد فسجد صلى الله عليه وسلم وقال رايت الحق تعالى وجل جلاله ب

حضرت محمد عليه السلام مقام قربه اولاشدي وجبرائيل عليه السلام بو مقام قربدور ديو اشارت ايلادوكي سجده ايلا ديب حضرت رسول صلى
دغي حقغه سجده ايلادي ب كوكل كوزي بيلا حق تعالى حضرتلرني كوردوم ديدوكي حالدر

Plate 36

THE SEVENTY THOUSAND VEILS (f. 42)

Beyond the seven Heavens, in infinite space, Mahomet now sees seventy thousand veils made of light, fire ruby, hyacinth, pearl, and gold. Each of the veils is guarded by seven divisions of angelic beings. The Prophet, guided by angels, passes through these seventy thousand veils in succession and sees the heavenly Throne, which is made of red hyacinth and so immense that compared with it the sky and earth would go unnoticed. A host of angels walks around the Throne singing litanies to the harp, night and day and in all languages, in honor of the Eternal, their voices as resounding as thunder. It is said that the angels that bear the Throne are closest to God. They praise Him tirelessly, professing their faith and begging pardon for the errors of the Believers.

The ritual of "circumambulation" goes back to the Bible. The Hebrews performed it around the altar (Psalms 25/26) and the Arabs around the Kaaba in Mecca (Koran II, 119; XXII, 27, 30). The great spiritual traditions practice the ritual in the same way, giving it the symbolic meaning of homage and sometimes even a cosmic significance, particularly in Islam, in which the seven circumambulations correspond to the number of the heavenly spheres.

As the Bible says that a veil conceals the Holy of Holies in the Temple of Jerusalem, so in Islam, the veil symbolizing revealed or communicated knowledge is rich in esoteric and mystical meaning.

Plate 35

THE FIVE DAILY PRAYERS (f. 38 v°)

Mahomet, prostrate, worships the Eternal. Then the Lord speaks to his Chosen One, enjoining him to teach his followers to recite fifty daily prayers. Bowing before the divine word, the Prophet (entirely surrounded by the prophetic flame) turns back to Moses (whose head only is circled by a fiery nimbus) and tells him of the order he has received. The Hebrew prophet, on the strength of his own experience among the people of Israel, advises him to reduce the number of prayers, which Mahomet does. On his request, the Eternal lowers the number at first to forty-five. Going back to Moses, the Prophet is once again advised to ask for a further reduction. The Lord lowers the number to forty, but Moses, thinking that forty daily prayers are still too many, sends Mahomet back a third time. Finally, after six supplications, the Eternal lowers the number to thirty, then to twenty, to ten, and at last to five. And, in His mercy, He adds: "I agree to repay as for fifty prayers any of your followers who repeat these five prayers in the ardor of their faith. . . ."

Though the Koran in fact sets down only three prayers, in daily life the rhythm of five prayers punctuates the Believer's day. From the high minaret of the mosque, the muezzin gives the call to prayer five times a day: at dawn, towards noon, in mid-afternoon, at sunset, and towards nightfall. These liturgical prayers demand a purification and ceremony fixed by tradition.

...ية النبي صلى الله عليه وسلم سبعين الف حجاب بعضها من نور وبعضها من
...بعضها من ياقوت وبعضها من لؤلؤ وبعضها من ذهب وفي كل حجاب سبعة...
...ملائكة وكل ملك منهم اخذ بيد النبي صلى الله عليه وسلم من ذلك الحجاب واو...
الي الحجاب الاخره

٣٣ 42

يه موسى للنبي عليهما الصلوة والسلام وسؤاله عنه بما قال له وأمر الله
ال أمرني بخمسين صلوة في خمسين وقت وأنه قال جعلتها فريضة عليك وعلى أمتـ
ال موسى ان امتك لا يقدرون عليها فارجع واسأله في التخفيف فسأله ذ
ن الله تعالى وهبه من الخمسين خمسة واربعين في مرات متعددة في كل مرة عشرة
فتقررت خمسة أوقات ٥

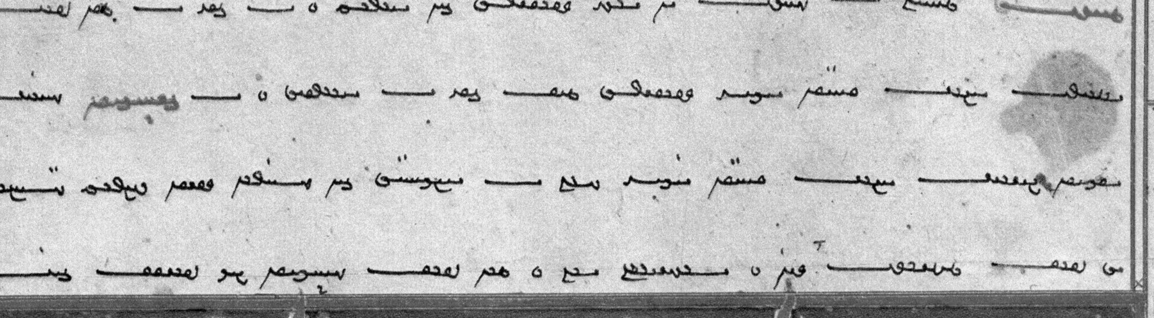

حضرت موسى عليه السلام حضرت محمد صلى الله عليه وسلمدن رؤيت الله ده نه امر اولندى وعندى سؤال ايلدوكده حضرت محمد ع م دخی اللی
وقت ده اللی بر کعت نماز امر اولندی دیدکده امتك بوکا قادر دکلدر داون دخی از اولماسنی دله دیوجك حضرت محمد ع م دخی از اولمانی
... بش وقت اوزره مقرر قلدوغی محلدر

Plate 38

HAVING REACHED THE THRONE, MAHOMET WORSHIPS GOD (f. 44)

Sitting down to remove his sandals, in order to be allowed to approach the Throne of God (*al-Arsh*), the Prophet hears a voice that says to him: "O Muhammad! do not remove your sandals, but let their blessed step attain my Throne." Having access to the Holy of Holies, he bows down, face to the ground (in this case to the golden clouds), saying: "Glory and praise!" As he is about to withdraw, Mahomet will see the Throne of Allah, in perfect clarity, held up by four angels.

In Islamic countries, custom says that a stranger must remove his shoes before crossing his host's threshold, an act which signifies that he has no legitimate claim to the ground he stands on. That is why even Believers must take off their shoes before they are allowed to walk into a mosque or Moslem sanctuary.

Plate 37

THE SEVEN HUNDRED THOUSAND TENTS

(f. 42 v°)

Mahomet, entirely surrounded by the prophetic flame, then sees seven hundred thousand tents arranged in a circle around the divine Throne, each tent as large as the earthly world. The space of a road fifty thousand years long separates them one from another. In each tent, fifty divisions of angels (some prostrate, some standing or sitting) worship God and recite litanies of the divine Names. The mention of many divisions of angels, in various places, reveals clearly the importance of these heavenly legions, whose numbers surpass our earthly systems of counting.

The tents surrounding the heavenly Throne suggest nomad encampments in the desert, at the center of which the tent reserved for God became a sanctuary, then a Temple, the midpoint of the world. According to tradition, the Throne of God (*al-Arsh*) was re-clothed each day in seventy thousand colors, and its luminous brilliance was such that no creature could look on it.

صول النبي صلى الله عليه وسلم وسجوده فوق العرش لله تبارك وتعالى

44 ٣

Plate 39A

CALLIGRAPHY PAGE (f. 47)

Plate 39

TO THE GARDENS OF PARADISE (f. 45 v°)

Leaving the divine Throne, Mahomet once again meets Gabriel, whose new mission is to show the Prophet the wonders that are reserved for Believers in Paradise. First his heavenly guide leads him to the shore of the Kawthar. Beside the water, the three gateways to Paradise, topped with domes of pearl, red hyacinth and emerald, make an extraordinary architectural composition, in which purity of line, luminosity of color, and richness of decoration combine with the sumptuousness of the polychrome faience fronts. The silt of the Kawthar is musk, the pebbles covering its bottom are red hyacinth. Its water is whiter than milk (Moslem tradition attributes an almost magical power to this color), and it is sweeter than honey and more fragrant than musk. On the bank, more numerous than the stars in the sky, are cups made of gold, silver, hyacinth, emerald, and fine pearls, so that those who wish to may relieve their thirst. According to a passage from the Koran (*sura* CVIII), this water had been given to the Prophet after the death of one of his sons, Abd Allah. Tradition says that whoever drinks of it will never suffer thirst again.

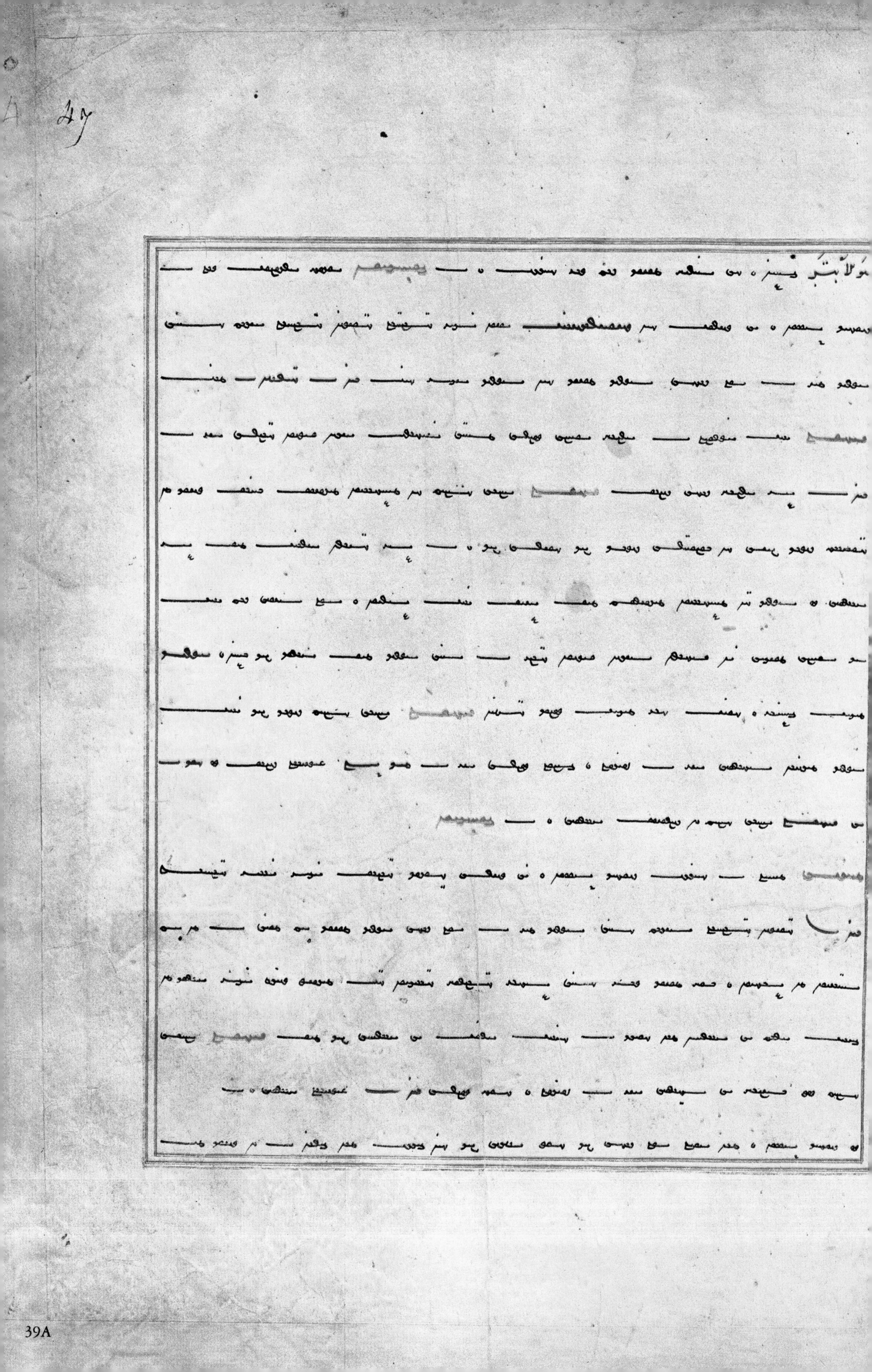

47

النبي صلى الله عليه وسلم لحوض الكوثر والقباب العالية التي هي من الياقوت
الأحمر وبعضها من الزبرجد وبعضها مخلوق من اللؤلؤ

Plate 41

THE HOURIS (f. 49)

In the gardens of Paradise, Mahomet, entirely encircled by the prophetic flame, riding the *Burāq* and accompanied by the angel Gabriel, sees a number of young and extraordinarily beautiful women, the *houris* (purified wives) which are promised to Believers. Some are joking and playing; others, climbing in the trees, are gathering bouquets; a few, seated on golden chairs, are conversing happily. Extraordinary birds show no hesitation in alighting on their heads. Several of the *houris* wear feathers in their hair. Streams of running water, shimmering with reflections, flow through this fairy-land where, for an endless springtime, an eternal sunlight reigns. In a universal melody, the chosen, the angels, the birds, and nature, enjoy the indescribable delights of Paradise.

The Koran (II, 23) evokes this Paradise, where the chosen dwell eternally, in terms of images: "Tell those who believe and have accomplished pious works that theirs will be the gardens where fresh streams flow. . . . In these gardens, they will find purified wives and will be immortal."

The Bible already had described Paradise as a place of delights, abundantly watered and planted with beautiful trees. For Islam also this Eden recalls the place where Adam and Eve lived before the Fall. It is described as a vast orchard, crossed by streams, where the palaces stand in which the chosen live with wives untouched by earthly taint. This description of a world whose pleasures are essentially earthly and material, has given rise to many questions. In truth, these allegorical scenes—intended for desert-dwellers—should be interpreted not according to the letter but as symbolic conceptions. Nevertheless, a number of Moslem mystics, rejecting the notion of such a Paradise, have seen eternal happiness only as the ecstatic contemplation of the divine Essence.

Plate 40

ARRIVAL IN PARADISE (f. 47 v°)

The angel Gabriel then brings the Prophet, followed by the *Burāq*, to Paradise. Gabriel knocks and the angel at the door (he is surrounded by a fiery nimbus) asks: "Who is it?" To which he replies: "I am Gabriel, and Mahomet, God's Envoy, is with me." Joyfully the angel greets Mahomet and the archangel and invites them to go into the gardens of Paradise.

Above the door that leads to Eden, the Moslem profession of faith is written in Kufic script. Spoken with sincerity, this religious declaration permanently joins the neophyte to the community of Believers. The content of the act of faith is a lapidary formula, the *shahada*, that appears in thirty verses of the Koran: "There is no other god but Allah," to which the Moslem adds, "and Mahomet is his prophet." For the Believer, this formula, which proclaims the Oneness of God, is also an act of worship. It is one of the five pillars of Islam.

سارؤيه النبي صلى الله عليه وسلم كرما في وسط الجنة وفيه جماعة
مِن الحور بعضهن جالسة على الكراسي وبعضهن تلعب مع بعضهن ٥

49

ي النبي صلى الله عليه وسلم الى باب الجنة وفتح الحاجب لبابها وتفرج

صلى الله عليه وسلم للجنة ٥

Plate 43

MEETING ONE OF THE FIRST HOLY WOMEN OF ISLAM (f. 51)

Proceeding to a palace that rises up in the midst of the gardens, the angel Gabriel, encircled by a fiery nimbus, guides Mahomet, mounted on the *Burāq,* toward a group of *houris,* among whom the Prophet sees one of the first noblewomen to embrace Islam, the wife of one of the "Companions of the Prophet."

The "Companions of Mahomet," who distinguished themselves in famous and fratricidal battles, figure among the first converts to Islam. They are particularly venerated by the Sunnites. One was named Talha; the text tells us that he was converted by his second wife, shown here wearing a Mongol-style crown (instead of the traditional feathered headdress worn by the other *houris*).

Plate 42

AMUSEMENTS OF THE HOURIS (f. 49 v°)

Moving among flower beds and blossoming trees, the Prophet, riding the *Burāq* and preceded by the angel Gabriel (who is surrounded by a fiery nimbus, his glittering wings spread in full flight), continues his promenade through the gardens, once again with *houris* wearing feathers in their hair, laughing and exchanging bouquets. Marvelous birds perch on the flower-laden branches of the trees. Some of the *houris* are mounted on camels, because each Friday, at the invitation of the Most-High, the chosen, followed by their wives, go across the skies to meet the Eternal beyond the heavenly Kaaba surrounded by praying angels.

The method of depicting the earth in these gardens owes to the Mongol school its superimposed longitudinal sections which simulate a gradual withdrawal toward the horizon. The vegetation has borrowed from Far-Eastern painting its stems drawn with a single brush-stroke and its bushes with their sinuous trunks and twisted branches covered with flowers.

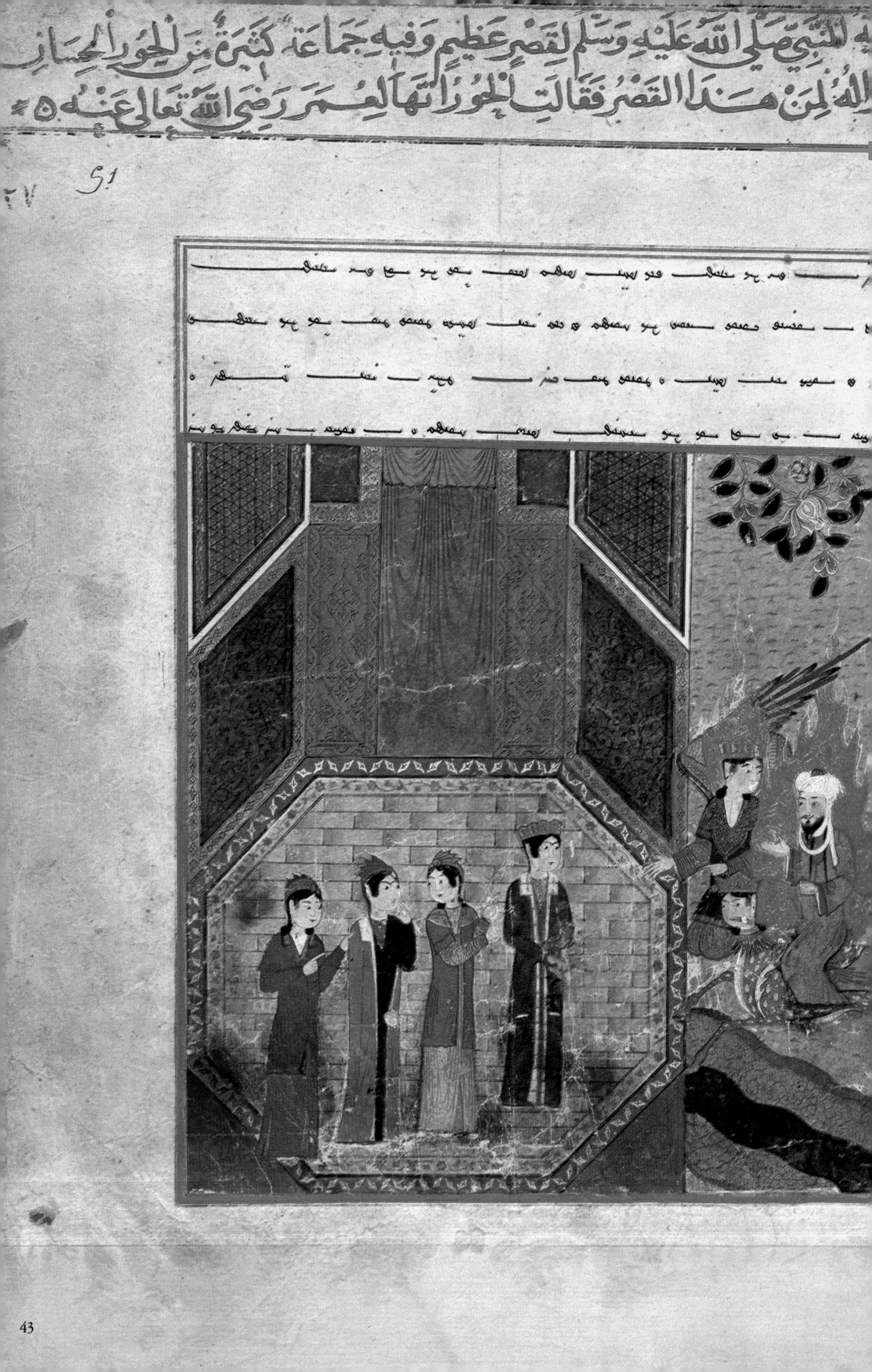

...ه النبي صلى الله عليه وسلم لقصر عظيم وفيه جماعة كثيرة من الحور الحسان

...اله لمن هذا القصر فقالت الحور انها لعمر رضي الله تعالى عنه ٥

٢٧

وُيتَه النَّبيِّ صلى الله عليه وسلم للحور في يوم الجمعة وهن راكبات على الجـ
تضحكن وترحب بعضهن على بعض وهن في السيرة

Plate 44

THE DOORWAY TO HELL (f. 53)

Leaving Paradise, the angel Gabriel then takes the Prophet (entirely enveloped in a fiery nimbus) toward the regions destined for the enemies of God, so that he may also see the seven Hells and the torments inflicted there. Reaching the doorway to Gehenna, Mahomet sees Mâlik, the prince who guards it. His aspect is terrifying. According to tradition, he has never smiled or exchanged a single word with anyone. Nevertheless, when Gabriel tells him the name of his illustrious visitor, he apologizes. At the Prophet's request, he blows on the fire of Hell, and the effect is so frightening that Mahomet feels an overpowering terror at it. In a number of places, the Koran mentions the fire of Hell. It is the supreme punishment inflicted by God on the damned. The Moslem Hell is made up of seven superimposed sections, of which the first, Gehenna, is reserved for Moslems guilty of grave errors; the others are destined for infidels.

In this painting, Mâlik is shown in the form of a demon with red face and body, dressed in a gold tunic covered with a red vest held in at the waist by a belt made of gold balls. He wears a gold crown on his head.

Plate 43A

CALLIGRAPHY PAGE (f. 51 v°)

...ـه باب جهنم وصورة مالك وقول النبي صلى الله وسلم يا مالك اضرم
جهنم دفعة واحدة وكيف اخذت الهيبة للنبي صلى الله عليه وسلم
وكذلك لجبريل عليه السلام ٥

53

Plate 46

THE PUNISHMENT OF EVIL-SPEAKERS (f. 55)

Pursuing his course, always guided by Gabriel, the Prophet, riding the *Burāq*, next sees black demons dressed in ochre or red loincloths who are cutting up the flesh of the damned and forcing them to eat it. These wretches are being punished for having hypocritically insulted and pitilessly spoken evil of Moslems. Still more than evil-speakers, the Koran condemns slanderers: "Accursed be the slanderers full of sin. . . . A cruel torment be upon them!" (XLV, 6–7).

Along with the other infernal spheres, this section of blazing fire is separated from the ones on either side of it by a shadowy realm, generally suggested by an atmosphere of deep black.

Plate 45

THE INFERNAL TREE (f. 53 v°)

Riding the *Burāq*, Mahomet, still led by the archangel Gabriel, sees a gigantic tree called *zekkum*. It fills a space as great as a road five hundred years long; its thorns are like spears; its fruit, bitterer than poison, has the form of the heads of lions, pigs, elephants, and other animals. The Koran (XXXVII, 60 ff.) mentions a "tree that grows in the depth of the furnace, whose fruit is formed like the heads of demons and will be eaten by the damned. . . ." The sinners who lie at the foot of this infernal tree have their tongues cut out by red demons; but no sooner is the amputation completed than they grow back again. During their earthly lives, these men failed to observe the precepts they taught, drinking wine and deliberately committing fornication and other perverse acts.

This section of Hell is guarded by a demon with blue body and red eyes, who rules over the red demons in purple or green loincloths who are engaged in torturing the damned (whose bodies are ochre-colored) in the midst of a blazing fire.

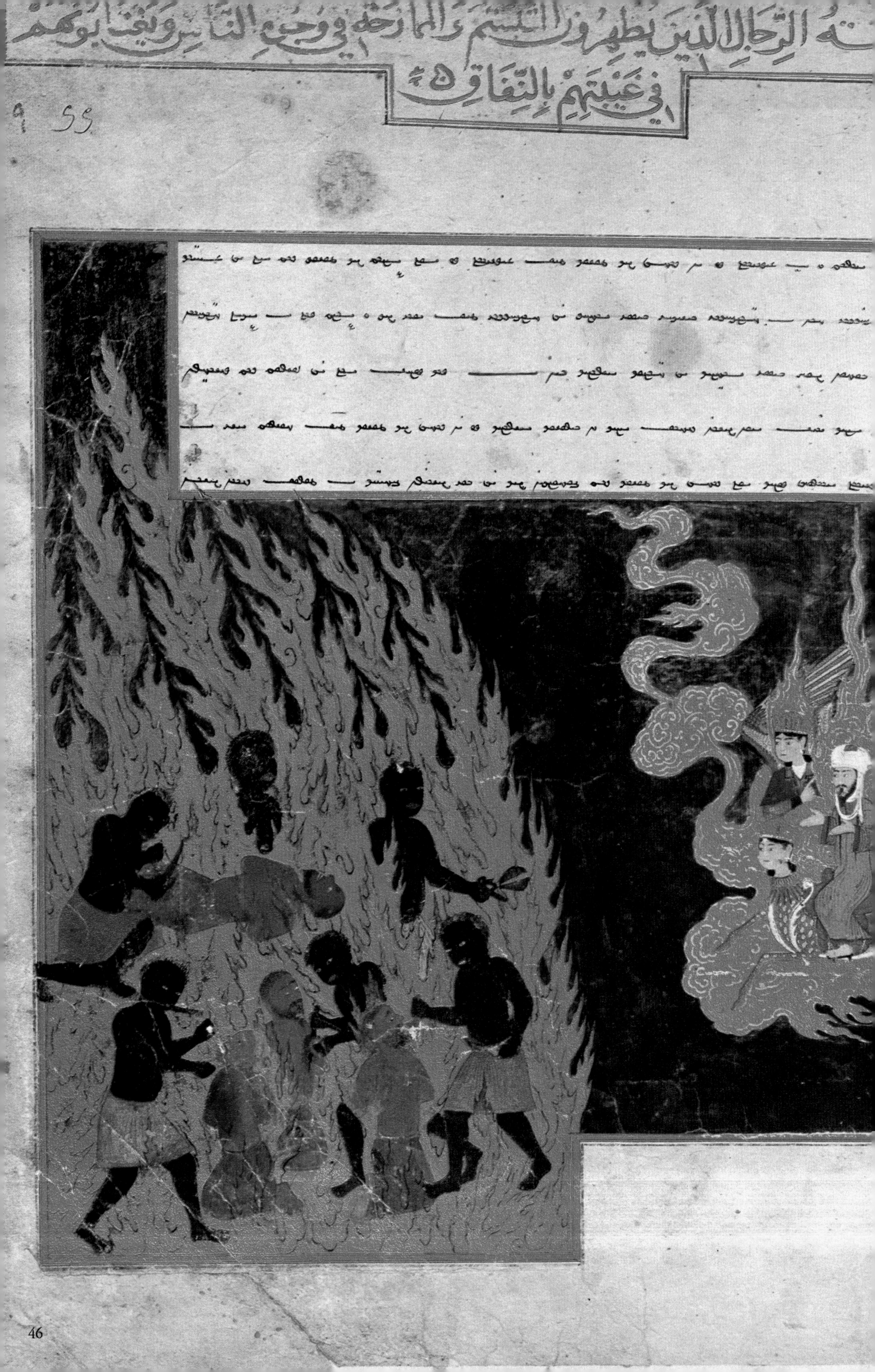

...ة الرجال الذين يظهرون التبسم والممازحة في وجوه الناس ويغتابونهم

في غيبتهم بالنفاق

صفة شجرة الزقوم التي شوكها مثل الرماح وثمارها رؤس العفاريت و

صفة الرجال الذين لا يعملون بعلمهم وينصحون الناس ويمنعونهم من العمل وهم يشتغلون به

Plate 48

THE SOWERS OF DISCORD (f. 57)

The Prophet, mounted on the *Burāq*, led by the angel Gabriel across another space of shadow, now watches the punishment reserved for those who falsely denounce Moslems to their oppressors, use violence to appropriate their goods and calumny to provoke quarrels, rivalries, and discords. The Koran, in some impetuous verses, violently stigmatizes false accusations, particularly those hurled against the apostles of Islam, and shows the terrible punishments that will strike those who fabricate deceitful accusations against the Believers.

Under guard of a green demon with hooked feet, red devils pierce the condemned with spears. The demon in charge of each infernal region is shown on the verge of the realm of shadow beside it.

Plate 47

GREED AND CUPIDITY (f. 55 v°)

After crossing another sphere of shadow, Mahomet, led by the angel Gabriel and riding his unusual mare, sees a gray demon with red, flaming eyelids holding a fork in his hand and breathing fire. This devil guards the greedy, who are immobilized by their own monstrously distended stomachs. Charity is a major virtue, manifested in the daily life of the Believer by alms-giving. Greediness and hoarding, the refusal to practice charity, implies in Islamic countries a state of impurity and unbelief whose gravity (emphasized in a dozen passages from the Koran, notably in *sura* IV, verse 41: ". . . those who are greedy, who spread greed among men, conceal the favor Allah has shown them: we have prepared for them a shameful torment") is such that it turns the Believer from the path of justice.

ه الرجال الذين يغتابون المسلمين عند الظالمين ليأخذوا اموالهم بالظلم
والذين يرمون الفتن بين المسلمين ٥

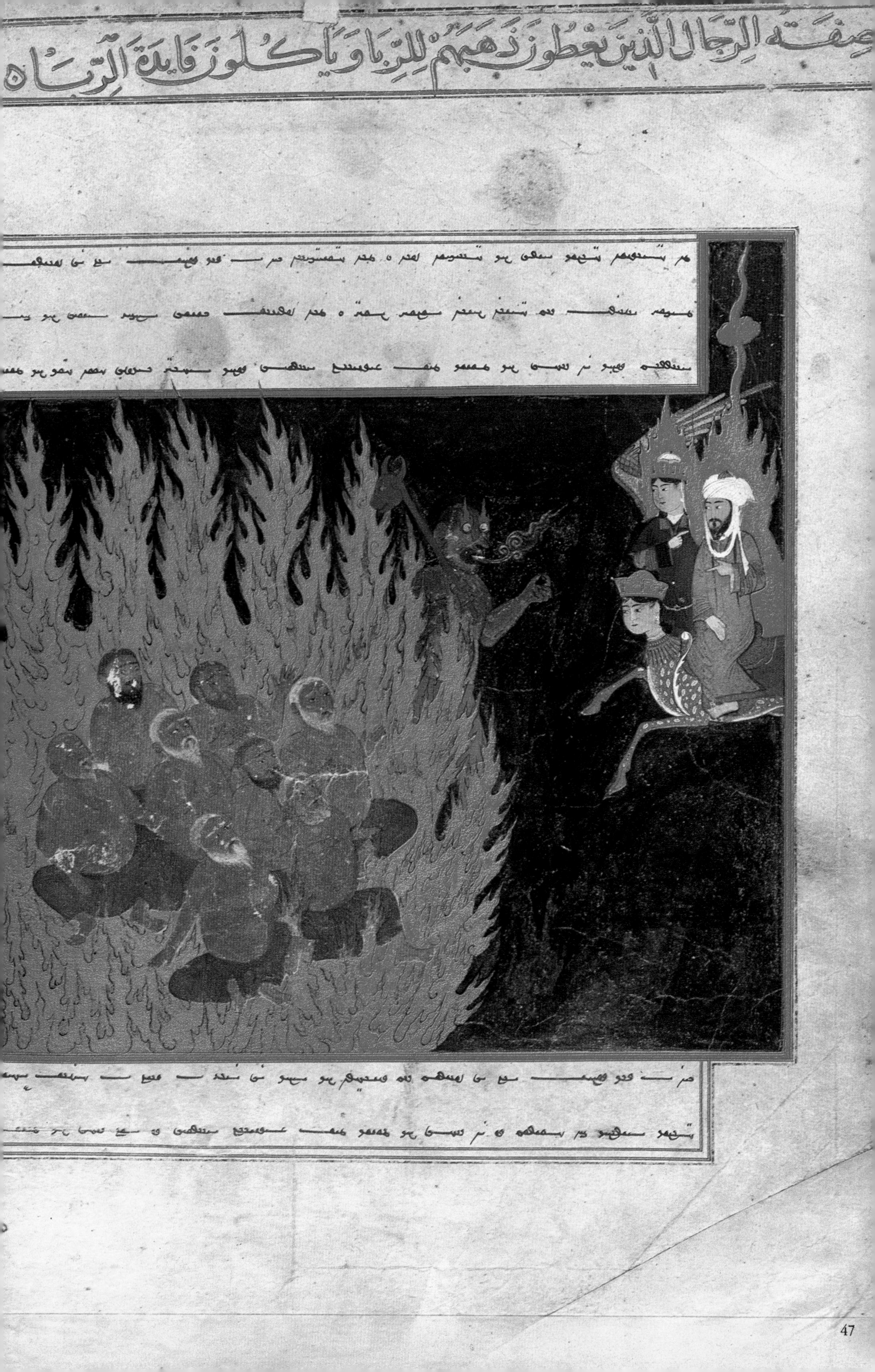

صفة الرجال الذين يعطون ذهبهم للربا و ياكلون فايدة الربا ه

Plate 50

THE SHAMELESS WOMEN (f. 59)

Having crossed another realm of shadow, the Prophet, mounted on the *Burāq* and guided by the angel Gabriel, contemplates the sufferings inflicted upon shameless women, particularly those who, by letting their hair be seen by strangers, encouraged criminal relations. These sinful women are hung up by the hair, and swirls of flame come from their nostrils. They are guarded by a brown demon with hooked feet, who is wearing ankle-bracelets, breathing fire, and holding a red fork in his hand.

Hair being one of a woman's principal weapons, the fact that it is hidden is a sign that she is unavailable or has already been chosen. In many places, the Koran (XXXIII, 55 and 59; XXIV, 59; and above all XXIV, 31) prescribes that woman wear a veil and be modest of demeanor: "Say to the believing women that they must lower their eyes, be chaste, and not display their adornment except what appears thereof. Let their veils cover their breasts! They should not display their adornment except to their husbands, or their fathers. . . ."

Plate 49

THE FALSELY DEVOUT (f. 57 v°)

Mahomet, mounted on his mare and accompanied by the angel Gabriel, here observes the punishment endured by those who simulated religious fervor in order to obtain temporal advantages. Hung from hooks over the infernal furnace, they are guarded by a violet demon with hooked feet, who holds a fork in his hand and breathes fire.

"Piety," says the Koran (II, 172), "does not consist in turning your face to the East or the West. The pious man is one who believes in Allah and in the Last Day, in the Angels, the Scripture, and the Prophets; who gives a portion of his wealth to neighbors, orphans, the poor, travellers, beggars; who frees his slaves; who says his prayers and gives alms; who fulfills the agreements he has contracted; who is patient in adversity, in suffering, and in the moment of danger: such are the Believers and the pious."

فة النساء التي ما سترن شعرها من غير ذي محرم وجرت بينهم امور
غير ملايمة

صفة الرجال الذين يصلون الصلوة رياء بغير إخلاص

Plate 52

THOSE WHO SQUANDER THE INHERITANCE OF ORPHANS (f. 61)

Continuing his infernal tour, guided by the angel Gabriel, Mahomet, mounted on the *Burāq*, sees red demons pouring a poisonous brew, extracted from the *zekkum*, down the throats of the damned. As soon as it is swallowed, the venomous liquid is excreted by the sinners, who are paying in this way for having embezzled, during their earthly life, the inheritance of orphans. They are guarded by a savage and snarling demon who holds a fork in his hand. The Koran (XVIII, 28) describes the torment inflicted on these sinners in precise terms: "We have prepared for the iniquitous a fire whose flames will encompass them. If they cry for relief, they will be relieved with water that is like molten brass.... What an evil drink! . . ."

Concerned with the condition of orphans, the Prophet recommended, in several Koranic verses, that they be treated like brothers and that their patrimony be scrupulously administered.

Plate 51

WOMEN OF LIGHT BEHAVIOR (f. 59 v°)

Further on, always guided by the angel across a space of shadow, Mahomet, riding the *Burāq*, sees women with tousled hair hung up by their tongues over a brazier, guarded by a green demon with hooked feet, breathing fire and holding a red fork in his hand. These women are paying for the mockery they were guilty of before their husbands, and for the licentious behavior they adopted during their earthly life, going out of the house without permission and engaging in dishonorable acts.

Islamic law, resting on certain Koranic verses, recommends that women act with the most perfect decency and modesty, in particular by wearing the veil and living a semi-cloistered life. This last prescription, which placed women in a state of inferiority, goes back particularly to a famous verse (XXXIII, 33): "Stay in your houses! Do not display your beauty in the old manner of the Gentiles. . . . Allah wishes only to keep uncleanness from you!"

صفة الرجال الذين يأكلون أموال الأيتام

يتيم مالين يين كشيلر قيامتده بوغازلرينه زقوم آقيدوب بويله عذاب اولنور انلرك صورتی بودر

صفة النساء التي تطول لسانهن على ازواجهن وتخرجن بغير اذنه وتشتغلن بالعمل الفاسد

شول عورتلر دورلر کیم ارلرینه دل اوزادور و اجازتسز طاشره چیقوب کورلر و فاسد عملگه مشغول اولورلر قیامت کونده بو یله عذاب ا

Plate 54

THE TORTURE ENDURED BY MISERS WHO FAILED TO PAY THE TITHE (f. 63)

Further on, led by the angel Gabriel and riding the *Burāq*, Mahomet sees a group of the damned with heavy millstones, symbolizing their wealth, hung around their necks. They are guarded by a black demon with red eyelids and a green face. Their riches, thrown into the infernal furnace, were transformed into the massive red discs we see here. In this way, the misers are paying, in particular, for not having given a tithe of their wealth. The Koran (III, 176), referring to misers, says specifically: "On the day of Resurrection they will wear around their necks what they hoarded in their lives."

The obligation of *zakât* (the tithe) comes from Islamic law. Once he is liberated from them, the Moslem can enjoy the goods of this world, as long as a portion is given back to Allah. In general, the payment is made proportional to each person's means. The sum is distributed to the poor, to slaves, sometimes to travellers or those to whom a debt of religious gratitude is owed.

Plate 53

THE PUNISHMENT RESERVED FOR ADULTEROUS WOMEN (f. 61 v°)

Mounted on his mare and guided by the angel Gabriel, Mahomet sees women with their hair loose about their shoulders hanging from hooks that go through their breasts. They are being tortured without surcease or mercy by a red demon with clawed feet who stirs the infernal fire with his fork. These women, not content with having violated conjugal faith during their earthly life, added to their crime by pretending that their children were legitimate. The children, fed and brought up by the deceived husband, became beneficiaries in his will along with the legitimate children. Instituted by the Koran (IV, 8, 37, 175), the system of inheritance was aimed essentially at preserving the rights of legitimate inheritors.

The familial morality of Islam, like that of Mosaic law (Job XXIV, 13–16), likens adultery to rebellion against God, and goes as far as to connect it with atheism. In the Middle Ages, fornication (*zinâ*) was subject to legal retribution; according to the gravity of the offense, the guilty might be condemned to a hundred lashes or to lapidation.

ـفة الرجال الذين ما اعطوا زكوة اموالهم

صفة النساء اللاتي يلدن الأولاد من غير ذي رحم وتدخلهم للميراث

Plate 56

PUNISHMENTS INFLICTED ON FALSE WITNESSES (f. 65, upper part)

Led by the angel Gabriel, Mahomet, riding the *Burāq*, sees a group of men with heads of pigs and asses' tails. Dried up by the scorching fire of Hell, they stick out long tongues in an effort to cool their thirsty lips. Large, pointed hooks come out of their mouths. Guarded by a red demon spitting fire, they are paying for having borne false witness (*zur*) during their earthly life.

Plate 56

PUNISHMENTS INFLICTED ON THOSE WHO PERFORMED NO GOOD ACTS (f. 65, lower part)

These wretches are by turns killed and brought back to life by red demons, who also cut out their tongues or slice them with swords. In Moslem ethics, good consists in doing what God ordains; doing what God forbids is evil; consequently, each act performed merits either reward or punishment. Hence the absolute obligation of obedience and total submission (*islam*) to Allah. Not to do good is thus a transgression of the Law, a grave moral failing, even a rebellion against the One God. The Koran confirms the condemnation of the guilty in these terms: "Those whose good deeds are few, they also will be the losers and will find immortality in Gehenna, their faces scorched by fire and their lips hanging open. . . ." (XXIII, 105 ff.).

Plate 55

SUFFERING INFLICTED ON HYPOCRITES AND FLATTERERS (f. 63 v°)

The Prophet, riding his mare and led by the angel Gabriel, sees a group of the condemned guarded by a hairy red demon who breathes fire. Their necks and wrists in chains, their feet shackled and their faces blackened, these unfortunate sinners are paying for their hypocrisy, either in embracing Islam for reasons of opportunism and thus being guilty of duplicity or deceit, or in offering flattering compliments and making a semblance of honoring and respecting the great while hating them in reality.

The form of torment inflicted on these condemned men is mentioned in the (Koran LXXVI, 4): "We have prepared chains, shackles, and a burning fire for the disbelievers." The Koran (III, 102) also alludes not only to radiant faces but to blackened ones, those of the miscreants and infidels, with whom our text associates the hypocrites. It should be noted that hypocrisy, in matters of religion, is considered a crime of the most extreme gravity.

صفة الرجال الذين يشهدون بالكذب والزور

65

صفة الرجال الذين اكرموا الامراء ري

Plate 58

TORTURES RESERVED FOR THE PROUD
(f. 67 v°)

Mahomet, mounted on his mare and led by the angel Gabriel, sees a number of boxes surrounded by flames. The proud and scornful are locked up in them and tormented by snakes (whose many teeth hold a terrible venom) and scorpions (whose numberless stingers discharge a violent poison) that go ceaselessly in and out. Questioned by the Prophet, Gabriel replies that these creatures were put there by God to punish the proud and scornful, who have acted coldly, and that these sinners will be tortured in this way by frightful and venomous reptiles and insects until the final day.

According to Islamic tradition, whoever bears within himself "a grain of mustard seed of pride" will not go to Paradise. In many places, the Koran condemns pride vigorously: "Allah loves not the proud" (XIV, 25), and "Do not turn your face from men! Do not walk the earth filled with disdain! Allah loves not the insolent full of their own vainglory" (XXXI, 17).

Plate 57

PUNISHMENTS INFLICTED ON DRINKERS OF WINE AND FERMENTED DRINKS (f. 65 v°)

Mounted on the *Burāq* as always, and guided by the angel Gabriel, Mahomet then sees certain of the condemned in chains and kneeling. Red demons pour a poison extracted from the bitter fruit of the *zekkum* (a kind of giant cactus) down their throats. In several places, the Koran speaks of this poison that is reserved for sinners in Hell: "The rebellious . . . will go through Gehenna . . . where they will drink boiling water and fetid liquids . . ." (XXXVIII, 55–57); "verily, o ye wayward! o deniers! you will eat of the trees of *zekkum*" (LVI, 51–52).

Having drunk wine and died impenitent, these wretches must undergo this tormet until the day of Resurrection. The prohibition against drinking fermented drinks (*khamr*) is precisely formulated in the Koran (V, 92). Already stated explicitly in several parts of the Bible (Leviticus X, 9; Judges XIII, 4; Numbers VI, 3–4), the prohibition against wine (and alcoholic drinks) seems connected mainly with its intoxicating properties. The prohibition against wine does not go back to the beginning of the Prophet's mission; in fact, the drink is celebrated in *sura* XVI, verse 69: "From the fruits of the palm and the grapes you obtain an intoxicating drink and excellent provision. . . ." But little by little Mahomet modified his attitude, perhaps because drunkenness was sometimes the cause of scandal, not only with the people but even among the Companions of the Prophet, and of errors committed during ritual prayer.

...تة الرجال الذين نفوسهم كبيرة واخلاقهم سيئة ويتكبرون
الخلق واذا ماتوا فان الله تعالى يعذبهم يوم القيمة بين العقارب والحيات

67

صفة الرجال الذين ماتوا ولم يتوبوا من الخ

LIST OF PLATES

NOTES

1. cf. Bibliography: Translations by Pavet de Courteille and by François Pétis de La Croix on which this discussion is largely based.
2. The date is not certain. Moslem writers place the Miraj between 617 and 624.
3. The spring of Zamzam which feeds the sacred well at Mecca (also known as the "well of Ishmael") is located to the southeast of the Kaaba, near the sanctuary of the Black Stone. Islamic tradition attributes the origin of this spring to the angel Gabriel who made a gift of it to Hagar and her son Ishmael when they were dying of thirst in the desert.
4. cf. Bibliography: M. Rodinson.
5. Latin MS 6064.
6. Latin MS 4072.
7. Chinese MSS Pelliot 2003, 2870 and 4523 in the Bibliothèque Nationale.
8. cf. Bibliography: *Les arts de l'Iran, l'ancienne Perse et Bagdad.*
9. *Ibid.*
10. *Ibid.*
11. cf. Bibliography: I. Stchoukine.
12. *Ibid.*
13. The manuscript actually contains 61 paintings (illustrating 61 episodes) but only 58 illuminated pages, since three pages have double illustrations.
14. Monique Maillard, "Essai sur la vie matérielle dans l'oasis de Tourfan pendant le haut moyen âge," *Arts asiatiques*, t. 29, 1973.
15. There is a perfect example of the nimbus in a Buddhist painting from Tuen-huang which shows two *vajrapani* (protectors of Buddhism) standing, surrounded by the flaming aureole and brandishing lightning (Bibliothèque Nationale, Chinese MS Pelliot 4031).
16. Jean-Paul Roux and Marie-Made-

leine Massé, "Quelques objets numineux des Turcs et des Mongols," *Turcica*, t. VIII, 1, 1976, pp. 28–57.

17. Jean-Paul Roux, "Le bonnet et la ceinture," *Turcica*, t. VII, 1975, pp. 50–64.

18. cf. "The Making of the Book," Stuart Cary Welch, *A King's Book of Kings*, 1972, pp 18–21.

SELECTED BIBLIOGRAPHY

Arts de l'Iran, l'ancienne Perse et Bagdad. Paris: Bibliothèque Nationale, 1938.

Binyon, L., J. V. S. Wilkinson, and B. Gray. *Persian Miniature Painting.* London, 1933.

Blochet, Edgar. *Catalogue des manuscrits turcs.* Paris: Bibliothèque Nationale, t. 1 (1932), 254–255.

Coran, Le (trans. Régis Blachère). Paris, 1966.

Courteille, Pavet de (trans.). *Mirâdj-nâmeh.* Paris, 1892.

During, J. *L'Islam, le combat mystique.* Paris, 1975.

Encyclopédie de l'Islam: Dictionnaire géographique, ethnographique et bibliographique des peuples musulmans. Paris-Leyden, 1927. [Cf. articles on isra, miradj, djanna (paradise), djahannam (hell), Idris, kibla, khamr (wine), and other Arabic words in text.]

Kühnel, E. *Miniaturmalerei im islamischen Orient.* Berlin, 1923.

La Croix, François Pétis de. "Traduction des inscriptions en langue turquesque qui marquent le sujet des soixante-et-quatre tableaux du Livre Leilet el mirage, écrit en caractère extraordinaire qui est de la Bibliothèque de Monseigneur Colbert, par La Croix, Secr. interprète du Roy." Bibliothèque Nationale, Turkish Manuscript Supplement 190 A.

Rodinson, Maxime. "Dante et l'Islam d'après des travaux récents," *Revue de l'histoire des religions*, t. 140 (1951), 203–235.

Sourdel, D. and J. "La Civilisation de l'Islam classique," *Collection les Grandes civilisations.* Paris, 1968.

Sourdel, Dominique. *L'Islam.* Paris, 1975.

Stchoukine, Ivan. *Les peintures des manuscrits tîmurîdes.* Paris, 1954.

Stchoukine, Ivan. *La peinture iranienne sous les derniers Abbâsides et les Il-Khâns.* Bruges, 1936.

Timoni, Alexandre. "Des anges, des démons, des esprits et des génies d'après les Musulmans," *Journal Asiatique* (1856), 147–163.

Toufy Fahd. "Anges, démons et djinns en Islam," *Sources Orientales* VIII (1971).

Wunderli, Peter. "Le Livre de l'Eschiele Mahomet," *Romanica helvetica,* vol. 77 (1968).